Frontier Forts and People Series

Only the Echoes: The Life of Howard Bass Cushing
Kenneth A. Randall

Howard B. Cushing
Howard Bass Cushing

Photo Courtesy of Army Military History Institute
Carlisle Barracks, Pennsylvania

FRONTIER FORTS AND PEOPLE SERIES

ONLY THE ECHOES

—— The Life Of ——
Howard Bass Cushing

by

KENNETH A. RANDALL

Yucca Tree Press

First printing   1995

Library of Congress Cataloging in Publication Data:

Randall, Kenneth A.

    ONLY THE ECHOES: The Life of Howard Bass Cushing

        1. Cushing, Howard Bass. 2. U. S. Frontier - History. 3. Civil War, U. S. - History. 4. Apache Indians - Warfare Against. 5. U. S. Cavalry - Indian Wars.
        I. Kenneth A. Randall. II. Title.

Library of Congress Catalog Card number: 95:061957

ISBN: 1-881325-19-9

Cover design by Fine Line Graphic Design

Dedicated to my wife, Peg,

for her patience.

ACKNOWLEDGMENTS

I began my search for the life and times of Howard Cushing in the National Archives, that vast treasure house of information concerning our nation's past. To DeAnne Blanton, who tirelessly sought information and filled my requests for obscure documents, I extend my heartfelt thanks. Kudos should be extended also to the staffs of the libraries of the University of Arizona, Arizona Historical Society and Pima Community College. My admiration goes to those who are so organized they can lay their hands on information that would take a layman much time and effort to locate.

To my good friend David Faust, Curator of the Fort Lowell Museum in Tucson, goes my gratitude for all his help in this seemingly long endeavor. His recall of sources was invaluable. Dave could, and should, write a book himself.

Margaret Zerwekh of Delafield, Wisconsin, a student of the Cushing family, was instrumental in supplying me with important data and avenues of research. Likewise thanks must go to the Darwin R. Barker Library of Fredonia, New York and the Chautauqua County Historical Society of Westfield, New York, for access to Cushing family papers.

My old friend and colleague Jean Wherely was kind enough to edit this work making sure all the 't's' were crossed and the 'i's' were dotted. Only to Jean, who has read, corrected and graded countless research papers in her high school English classes, would I trust to make sure my less than perfect grammar was correct.

Last, and by far not the least, many thanks must go to my good wife Peg for her patience and understanding. She gritted her teeth and tiptoed around the clutter sometimes attendant to research. Repressing her strong instinct for order, she never once attempted to make neatness out of a mess.

To you the reader, I present my efforts.

TABLE OF CONTENTS

ILLUSTRATIONS and MAPS

Photographs

Maps

INTRODUCTION

History is replete with individuals whose fame, like a stellar nova, shone brightly for a brief period of time and then faded into obscurity, soon to be forgotten. Such a man was Howard Bass Cushing. Serious students of Southwestern history will immediately recognize his name, but others may have heard of him only in passing. His final scout in southern Arizona has been immortalized in Dan Thrapp's classic work, *The Conquest of Apacheria*, and it is through this venue that most people are aware of his name. However, every man who has ever committed a noble act has a past that preceded such a deed and that period of his life should be examined to determine those factors which shaped his being.

Cushing's rise from the rank of private in the Civil War to his almost heroic status as a cavalry officer in the American Southwest was not without its adventurous and, at times, seamy side. The cavalry has been overdramatized by modern film makers into a romantic life-style by portraying them charging overwhelming numbers of Indians, with sabers flashing in the sun. In reality, the life of the horse soldier was tedious, boring and, at times, extremely dangerous. His tenure in the Southwest was endangered not only by his enemy, the Apache, but also by insects, serpents, disease, and the harsh climate itself. The common soldier often had a checkered past, the army being an avenue of escape. Some joined in the hope of a better life, while still others, with no marketable skills to offer the avenues of commerce, enlisted to spend a brief period in relative security or to make the military a career. The soldier of the Southwest in the period following the Civil War differed somewhat from his counterpart in that conflict. Although many members of the military from 1861-1865 were those who had volunteered out of patriotic zeal, others, unable to find or afford paid substitutes, were drafted. The post-war army consisted only of volunteers, whatever their reasons may have been for joining.

With great expectations I began a long and tedious search for the details of Howard Cushing's life. Disappointments mounted quickly as I learned my subject had left very little recorded history of his own — few letters and no diaries. It soon became evident that it would be necessary to piece together his life through official documents, records, and the recollections of contemporaries. His service as a private in an Illinois artillery unit in the early stages of the Civil War could be followed only through the movements of his unit. In his battery's official reports Cushing's name appears twice —once when he joined and again when he left. Only when he became an artillery officer in the regular army does his name appear in the report of his battery and his presence can be attributed to specific actions. Even then details are obscure. After he became a cavalry troop commander, it was possible to link his name with actual movements and engagements. Howard Cushing lived just past his thirty-second year and, except for those impacted by his actions, he was hidden from public acclaim by the nature of his assignments.

Cushing's first military experience was as a private with a volunteer artillery regiment in 1862. Although the descriptions of the types of field pieces used in the Civil War may seem too detailed, they were an important part of his early army experience and totally unrelated to his later function as a cavalry officer. The mounted units he was to command in the Southwest had a different function than cavalry during the Civil War. Roaming over larger distances and contacting the enemy only sporadically, the post-war cavalry abandoned the tactics of reconnaissance, the eyes and ears of a larger militia. Instead, they became the initial striking force, the point, so to speak, in the tedious effort to subdue the Indians during the second half of the nineteenth century.

The nineteenth century has been described as the end of the middle ages in medicine. Likewise, the horse was the principal mode of transportation whether ridden astride or pulling some sort of wheeled vehicle. The weapons of the day can in no way be compared to those of modern times. Slow muzzle velocities and the use of black powder, the propellant that resulted in much smoke and begrimed the face of the marksman, were in the technological forefront. We must also forget the 'Hollywood Regiments' which, in many ways, do not realistically represent the actual conflict between Indians and soldiers. (As an aside, forget those silly yellow kerchiefs worn in the movies and never worn by the real soldiers they attempted to portray.) Another often overlooked tactic of cavalry warfare was the use of only seventy-five percent of the force present to actually engage the enemy. For every quartet of horsemen, three dismounted to fight while the fourth took the reins of the horses and led them rearward out of the range of gunfire.

No man alive today can accurately describe the concussion felt in the chest by the muzzle blast of cannon at Shiloh. No one living can sense the feeling of apprehension and perhaps fear the cavalryman felt as he and his comrades rode through a narrow canyon, looking up on all sides for any sign of an Indian attack. My hope is that this work will assist the reader in understanding at least one of these men.

Ken Randall
Tucson, December 1995

PROLOGUE

What follows is the story of a man, unknown to most but considered by others a hero. Howard Bass Cushing was an army officer stationed in New Mexico and Arizona Territories following the Civil War. Tenacious to the core, he was feared by his enemies and lauded by the Anglo and Hispanic settlers of the Southwest. If it is true that a man's character is shaped in part by the time and external circumstances in which he lived, it is then pertinent that the historic events of his lifetime be recalled.

Cushing's military career began during the Civil War, that great strife which, for a period of four years, tore at the heart of the nation. We will later explore his rise from the ranks of private in a state militia to that of an officer in the regular army. Although volumes have been written about the battles that took place between 1861-1865, Cushing's involvement in these events will be recorded when we more closely examine his life.

Following the war, internal struggles began to emerge within the nation. The untimely assassination of President Abraham Lincoln altered forever the policies of bringing the nation together after this splintering conflict. Many in the north were opposed to any type of appeasement towards the rebel states. A most highly unlikely successor to the office of Chief Executive was Andrew Johnson. The office of Vice-President was strictly political, held in low esteem and the candidate was chosen not on ability but rather on his capacity to garner votes in a particular segment of the population. Thus, upon his election on the Republican ticket, no one expected Johnson to hold the highest office in the land. To his credit, Johnson tried to carry forth Lincoln's plans for reconciliation with the South, but he ran head-on into a group of Congressmen called 'the Radicals.' Their aim was to punish the rebel states and exclude from office any Southerners who had supported the Confederate cause. Also, perhaps because Johnson himself was a Southerner and former slave holder, other members of Congress did not trust his efforts to carry out Lincoln's principles in bringing the nation together. These differences finally led to a vote of Impeachment in the House and a trial in the Senate. After deliberations, which virtually brought to a halt the business of the nation, President Johnson was acquitted by a vote of 32-19.

Meanwhile, the South was in turmoil. Unscrupulous politicians known as Carpetbaggers invaded the area, promising newly freed slaves power over their former masters in exchange for such favors that would line the pockets of these individuals. During this time Federal troops had to act as an army of occupation and on many occasions were called out to quell disturbances and rescue Republican leaders from harm. In 1871 troops were called out more than two hundred times and soldiers were stationed in every large southern city and seaport.

While the nation's attention was drawn to the squabbles in Congress and the problems of Reconstruction in the South, changes were taking place west of the Mississippi. The long-existing question of what to do about Native Americans was yet to be settled. The Homestead Act of 1862 opened new lands for settlement and these pioneers, many of them Civil War veterans, were clamoring for a solution to the Indian problem. Most felt that such diverse cultures could never live in harmony. Americans, nationwide, espoused the feeling that only the complete subjugation of the various warlike tribes was the answer to this vexing problem. It was estimated that between 1846 and 1861 Indians had killed approximately four hundred settlers and stolen one million dollars worth of livestock. The

Policy of Concentration in 1851 determined that the various tribes would allow settlers free passage through their lands and the Indians would confine their hunting to certain areas. However, game animals such as buffalo knew no boundaries and the policy failed with the discovery of gold in Colorado.

In 1867, a Peace Commission replaced the Policy of Concentration with one of placing all Indians on reservations and the control of these sites was to be overseen by the Bureau of Indian Affairs (BIA). The BIA, established in 1824 as part of the War Department, was transferred in 1849 to the Department of the Interior. The Bureau was notorious from the outset for corruption. Civilians in the East were ill-equipped to understand this ever increasing problem for those residing in the West. Positions of Indian Agent, those persons chosen to represent the BIA on the reservations, were readily bought and sold. This position was used by these individuals to line their own pockets by cheating the Indians out of the food and goods to which they were entitled or substituting items of very poor quality and keeping the ill-gained profits for themselves. A member of President Grant's cabinet, William Belknap, was accused of accepting bribes for appointments to various Indian Agent posts. Coupled with this was the fact that many Indians rejected the reservation concept and refused to live in the lands set aside for them. Treaties and promises were broken by Indians and whites alike.

In the Southwest, matters had become especially critical in the years following the Mexican War. Settlers poured into the area to search for gold and silver. Many settled on small ranches, raised paltry herds of cattle and practiced subsistence farming. Indian leaders, such as the Apache Cochise, tolerated these newcomers as merely a nuisance, but became alarmed when their numbers grew.

The Butterfield Stage Line had regular runs through Apache lands prior to the Civil war, and the Apaches supplied some of the most remote stage stations with hay and firewood. This rather tense coexistence was shattered by what was to become known as 'The Bascom Incident.' A small boy, Felix Ward, was kidnapped from his home near Patagonia, Arizona, by Indians. This was not an uncommon occurrence and those so captured were often held as slaves. Lieutenant George Bascom and a detail of men met with the Apache leader Cochise in the vicinity of Apache Pass, Arizona, in an effort to effect the release of the young lad. Cochise protested that his tribe, the Chiricahua Apaches, was innocent but that he would attempt to find the boy and return him to his parents. Here Lieutenant Bascom erred, informing Cochise that he could not be trusted and would remain a prisoner of the army until the boy was reunited with his family. Eyewitnesses reported that the Apache leader slashed the rear of the tent where the meeting was being held and escaped on foot under a hail of bullets. Bascom held some of Cochise's followers as hostages against young Ward's return. The next day Cochise attempted to take as prisoners employees of the Butterfield Stage Line. In the ensuing fray the station-keeper was killed by the Indians and a hostler was killed accidentally by soldiers from inside the station. Bascom, in retaliation, hanged some of his Indian prisoners. The Indians reacted by raiding nearby ranches, killing settlers and stealing cattle; thus the depredations began. With the withdrawal of Federal troops to the East to fight the Civil War, the protection of the Southwest was left to the California Volunteers, a state militia whose primary assignment was to halt the invading Confederate Army moving west from Texas. Until the conclusion of the war, the Indians of the Southwest had almost a free rein at raiding both north and south of the Mexican border.

In 1868, in an effort to economize and reduce the debt of the recent war, Congress passed the Army Reorganization Act. The already overtaxed manpower of the military was reduced to twenty-five regiments of infantry and ten regiments of cavalry. This left twenty-five thousand men to occupy the South, man coastal fortifications and put down Indian disturbances in the West from Canada to Mexico. With little knowledge of Indian warfare and tactics, Second Lieutenant Howard Cushing reported to Fort Union, New Mexico, on September 16, 1868. In less than three years he would be dead, felled by an Apache bullet.

CHAPTER I

THE CUSHING FAMILY

No study of a man could begin without at least a casual survey of his origins, those family factors which are so instrumental in the development of one's personality. Family background is as important, if not more so, as the socioeconomic conditions that exist during a lifetime.

Howard Cushing's grandfather, Zattu, born in 1771, left the place of his birth, Plymouth, Massachusetts, and emigrated to Ballston Spa, New York.[1] Such a move was not unusual in the years following the Revolutionary War. The returning veterans found that debts had accrued in their absence and that creditors were unwilling to accept the 'worthless Continental currency' with which the soldiers were paid.[2] Thus, it seems natural that Zattu, although too young to have fought in the recent war, would make the trek into what was then considered the western wilderness. It is likely that Zattu reached Ballston Spa sometime prior to 1795, the year of his marriage to Miss Rachel Buckingham.[3] Zattu is next found in 1799 when he oversaw the construction of a ship, *Good Intent*, being built on an island near Erie, Pennsylvania.[4] Zattu's occupation in Plymouth was possibly that of ship's carpenter.

In 1805, Zattu and Rachel settled in what is now Fredonia, New York. By this time, the family had grown to five children, one of whom was Milton Buckingham Cushing, Howard's father. Fredonia, slightly inland of the Lake Erie port of Dunkirk, was a natural place for a ship's carpenter to put down permanent roots. Setting up housekeeping in a log cabin, the Cushings soon became leading members of the community. Zattu was so respected that he was appointed Associate Judge of the Niagara County Court.[5] Although the sessions were held in Buffalo, Zattu attended all terms and became the leading member, presiding "at the most important trials."[6]

In 1811, Chautauqua County was created from a part of Niagara County. Zattu Cushing, on the basis of his experience, was immediately chosen as Chief Judge of this new political subdivision.[7] It was said that Zattu settled more cases in private than in the courtroom.[8]

Retiring from the court in 1825, Zattu turned his energies to new endeavors. In October of that year the Erie Canal opened, connecting the western part of the state of New York with the seaport of New York City. Seizing this new opportunity, in 1826, Zattu and his neighbors built a barge for use on the canal. Appropriately this vessel was named *Fredonia Enterprise*. The barge was towed to Buffalo and from there sent across the canal, its hold laden with the first wheat grown in the new country for export. A goodly portion of that first cargo was grown on Zattu's farm.[9] Until his death in 1839, Zattu engaged in business and enjoyed the benefits of a fruitful life. At the next term of court after his death, a portrait of Zattu was hung in the courthouse over the bench occupied by the judges. His contemporaries said that Zattu possessed "restless energy and indomitable will."[10] These same traits were inherited by his grandson.

By the time of Zattu's death, his son, Milton, had grown to adulthood and graduated from Hamilton Literary and Theological Institute (now Colgate University) with a degree of Doctor of Medicine.[11] A slender, nervous man, the duties of a physician were "too exacting for his health."[12] After a few years of not-so-successful practice in Zanesville, Ohio, he became a merchant in that city, as well as in Columbus, Ohio. While in Zanesville, he married Abigail Tupper, whose grandfather had been a general in the Revolutionary War.[13] In 1833 Abigail died leaving Milton with four children. Sadly, all of the children born of this marriage died in early adulthood. Two of the daughters lived only long enough to marry, and the oldest son Benjamin, a law partner of Salmon B. Chase, died in his mid-twenties.[14]

Although Milton was greatly saddened by his wife's death, he had four young children to raise and a business to run. He soon married again, this time to Mary Barker Smith, daughter of a prominent Boston family. The couple met while Mary was visiting relatives in Columbus. She was a "lineal descendent of John Alden" and other Boston persons of historical note.[15] Mary was born in 1807 and married to Milton at the age of 29 in 1836. He had been a widower for three years and Mary instantly became the stepmother of four children. Mary was described as having a "splendid physical and mental constitution and fortunately endowed with a passionate love for life in a free and open atmosphere."[16]

The eldest son of this marriage was born in 1837 and named for his father, Milton Buckingham Cushing, Jr. Shortly after Milton's birth, the Cushings moved to the wilds of Wisconsin and settled in the village of Milwaukee. In 1838, Milwaukee's population was eight hundred people living on both sides of the Milwaukee River.[17] Into this hot, mosquito infested environment, Howard Bass Cushing entered the world on August 22, 1838. Mary was up and about three days later.[18]

In 1839, the family moved a few miles north of the site of present-day Waukesha to what is now Delafield, Wisconsin. Here were born Alonzo, on January 19, 1841; William on November 4, 1842; and Walter, who died in infancy. Alonzo

Delafield, Wisconsin area.

was to become heroic as the commander of the artillery battery which was the focal point of Pickett's famous charge at the Battle of Gettysburg. He was killed while repulsing Lee's last gasp attempt to salvage a victory. William was a naval officer during the same war and his deeds have been memorialized in *Lincoln's Commando*, by Ralph Roske and Charles Van Doren.

After arriving in their new home, Dr. Cushing's health seemed to be invigorated. Shortly thereafter, Delafield Township was set apart from the town of Nemahbin. The town name was changed to Delafield in 1843 by the legislature. Doctor Cushing, having already been Justice of the Peace, assumed the office of chairman of the township's first Board of Supervisors. He performed his duties "with charm and a sort of fatigued dignity."[19] By 1844, however, the fresh air and sunshine which had seemed to enhance Doctor Cushing's well-being became too strenuous and the family moved again, this time to Chicago. Here, in a home on the waterfront, Doctor Cushing resumed the practice of medicine. The last Cushing child, Mary Isabel, was born here. Although her exact birth date is unknown, the Fredonia, New York census of 1850 lists her age as four, meaning her birth year was 1846.[20]

Doctor Cushing's health worsened again by the fall of 1846 and it was decided he should travel to a warmer climate to regain his strength, leaving the family behind in Chicago. Although there is no proof, Doctor Cushing may have suffered from tuberculosis. In November of that year he set out to visit his cousin, Judge L.S. Houghton, of Vicksburg, Mississippi.[21] The change in climate seemed to help and in the spring of 1847 he started north to rejoin his family. He stopped in Columbus, Ohio, to arrange for his son Benjamin's partnership with Chase. This being done, he set out to rejoin Mary and the children. In Gallipolis, Ohio, he contracted a cold which developed into pneumonia and died alone in a hotel room in that city. Upon receiving the news of her husband's death, Mary gathered her children around her, went to Gallipolis and from there accompanied her husband's body to Fredonia, New York, for interment. Surprisingly, Doctor Cushing left no provision for his widow and children.[22]

In the summer of 1847, Mary Cushing and her children moved from Chicago to Fredonia. She settled in a house on

Green Street, the Cushing family home being inhabited by one of Zattu's other children.[23] The town of Pomfret assessment rolls indicate that in 1849 Mary owned a one-eighth-acre lot valued at fifty dollars.[24] Mary and the children appear in the 1850 Federal Census although, the last name is spelled 'Cushion.'[25]

Fredonia, New York area.

In order to provide for herself and the children, Mary started a private school in her home and the income provided for the needs of the family. The New York State Census of 1855 reported Mary residing in a frame house valued at five-hundred dollars. The same census names her daughter Mary as the only child living at home.[26] Logs of the Fredonia Academy note Milton and Howard enrolling for the first term of 1852. Howard is also listed as attending the second term in 1853. The records indicate that Howard studied arithmetic, algebra, grammar and philosophy in 1852 and in 1853, and used *Davies Arithmetic*, *Weld's Grammar* and *Smith's Philosophy* as textbooks for four weeks. Alonzo and William enrolled for the third term in 1853 but Milton and Howard do not appear again in any school records.[27]

The two older boys worked at various odd jobs to supplement the family income. Milton worked on an uncle's farm for about a year and then moved to Fitchburg, Massachusetts, to work in a pharmacy owned by a relative.[28] Howard, meantime, worked in the office of the local newspaper, *The Censor*, for about a year but left to take a position on a Boston newspaper, a job presumably obtained for him by someone in his mother's influential family. Some accounts state that at the age of eighteen, in 1856, he became homesick and returned to Fredonia.[29] However, the Boston City Directory of July 1859 reports him living at Number 4 Hudson Street.[30] Sometime after July of 1859, he moved to Chicago where he took a position as a reporter for a local newspaper, *The Farmer's Advocate*.[31] In the meantime, Alonzo had received an appointment to West Point and William, likewise, to the Naval Academy. Both appointments were procured by various members of their mother's family. William attended Annapolis until a prank led to his dismissal. (A bucket of water was perched on top of a door left slightly ajar. Unfortunately, the individual for whom the prank was intended was not the first person through the door but rather it was the Spanish instructor.) William was later reinstated in the Navy through the efforts of Admiral Joseph Smith, another of Mary's relatives.[32]

With the outbreak of the Civil War in 1861, many young men answered the call of Present Lincoln to serve their country. On March 24, 1862, Howard B. Cushing enlisted as a private in Company B, First Illinois Light Artillery and left the city for an inauspicious beginning to his military career.[33] (See Appendix, Exhibits A, B, C.)

CHAPTER II

THE FIRST ILLINOIS
LIGHT ARTILLERY

Cushing's choice of a branch of the military was probably not just by chance. Residing in Chicago at the time, far from any ocean, it seems most likely he would not have chosen the navy, the option of his brothers, Milton and William. Although there was naval activity during the Civil War, the conflict was primarily a ground war between the two opposing armies. Howard's brother, Alonzo, had been appointed to the Fourth United States Artillery Regiment upon his graduation from West Point. Howard, too, enlisted in an artillery unit, the First Illinois Light Artillery Regiment, a volunteer group from the state originating in Chicago. Regiments of this type were recruited and supported initially by the city or state of their origin and quickly assimilated into a regular army corps. Cushing himself says that he enlisted, "for 3 months at the first call of the President," but no confirmation can be found for this time period.[1] The first record of any service to be found in the Battery Muster Roll for Battery B, First Illinois Light Artillery, indicates he "enrolled and mustered in at Chicago, March 24, 1862, for three years."[2]

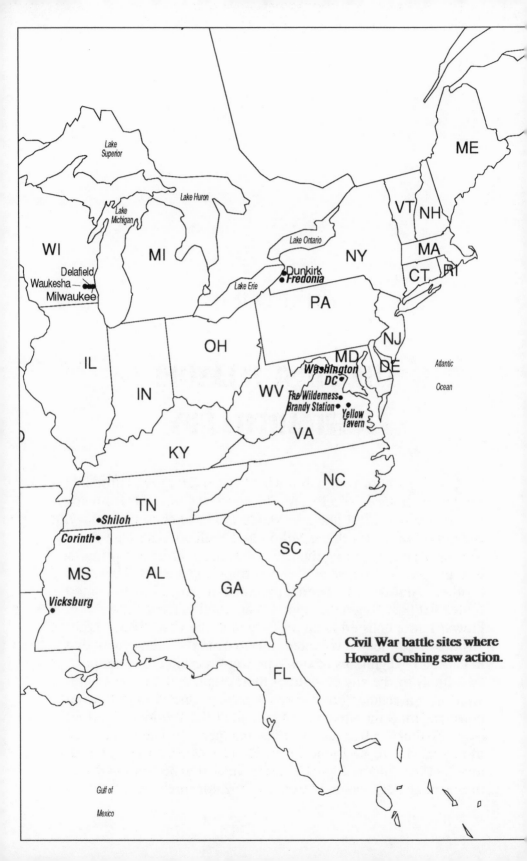

Civil War battle sites where Howard Cushing saw action.

The use of artillery in nineteenth century warfare is best expressed by General Henry Hunt.

> Infantry and cavalry require the aid of artillery for specific purposes: to destroy walls, earthworks and other means of cover; to set fire to, or render untenable farm buildings, villages, woods and other lodgments, etc. Its presence alone, if known to be powerful, often prevents the enemy from resorting to such defenses. Thus set free for its primary objectives, the artillery is used in the open field to commence battles, to prepare the way and aid in attacks, to protect the movement of our own troops, and to hinder those of the enemy, to pursue and prevent the enemy from rallying, or to cover our own retreat.[3]

The common artillery piece in most light batteries was the Napoleon twelve-pounder with a muzzle bore of 4.62 inches.[4] While the Union Army manufactured these guns from brass, the Confederates, for the most part, lacked this metal and were forced to make these pieces from cast iron with a reinforced breech. In most instances, the brass guns the rebel army possessed were those captured from opposing forces. The twelve-pounder could fire solid shot to a maximum range of 1,680 yards but its most effective use was as, in what would be called today, an anti-personnel weapon in close support of infantry.[5] However, company records of Battery B indicates that two sections of the battery (two guns per section) consisted of six-pounder field guns and one section (two guns) of twelve-pounders.[6] Six-pounders, with a muzzle bore of 3.67 inches, had a maximum range of 1,523 yards firing solid shot but were used primarily to repel the attack of enemy foot soldiers.[7] Although the practice of having different types of guns in a battery seems to be a common one, it also had one great disadvantage, that of supply within the battery. For example, if the ammunition for the twelve-pounders was exhausted, these guns were rendered useless because resupply could not be accomplished from within the same battery. During the heat of battle, batteries operated almost independently, so it was possible that from one-third to two-thirds of a battery could be out of action.

Although Battery B did on occasion fire solid shot, *i.e.*, during the siege of Vicksburg, its most telling weapon was that of canister. Canister consisted of a tin can filled with small cast iron or lead balls placed in dry sawdust. When fired, the balls scattered across the field much like a giant shotgun, tearing into the ranks of advancing enemy troops.[8] These rounds were most deadly against the battle tactics of the 1860s which called for suicidal charges across open ground against the fortified lines of the foe.

Cushing's own recounting of his Civil War experiences begins with "Grant's movements on the Tennessee River," and his first battle was the terrible carnage at Shiloh.[9] The exact date he joined Battery B is unclear, for reports from the battery and the regimental history indicate only his date of enlistment.[10] Sometime between March 24 and April 5, 1862, Private Howard Cushing arrived at the camp of Battery B. The unit joined the Fifth Division of Major-General U.S. Grant's Army of the Tennessee, commanded by Brigadier-General William T. Sherman, on the eve of the unexpected Battle of Shiloh.[11] The Fifth Division consisted of four brigades of infantry. Each brigade consisted of three infantry regiments (total manpower - 7,180), three artillery batteries (eighteen guns, total manpower - 330), and two companies of cavalry (total manpower - 304).[12] Sherman was later to say that one of these cavalry companies, Thielman's Brigade, was no more than, "mounted orderlies."[13]

Grant had intended resting his army at Pittsburg Landing, Tennessee to await the arrival of Don Carlos Buell and his Army of the Ohio. When the two armies had massed they were to march on the Confederate forces gathering at Corinth, Mississippi. Albert Sidney Johnston, the rebel commander, aware that Grant was waiting for reinforcements, decided to attack before Buell could arrive. At 4:00 a.m. on April 6, the Confederates launched their attack on the unwary Union lines. Sherman's Fifth Division was camped in what was to become the center of the battle, and Battery B was placed "on the brow of a hill in the rear of Shiloh Church."[14] Shiloh, meaning peace, would seem to be a proper name for a church but not for a battle. The Southern armies called it the Battle of Pittsburg Landing. The battle tactics determined that the center of the

Federal line would bear the brunt of the attack. Firing round after round of canister, Battery B repulsed successive charges of enemy infantry and "line after line of grey and butternut troops was smashed to pieces in vain."[15] Cushing recalls repulsing "the charge of three regiments of infantry supported by three batteries and 1,000 cavalry."[16] His commanding officer, Captain Samuel Barrett, more conservatively reported, "Here we were charged by several regiments of rebel infantry."[17]

About 9:15 a.m., a Confederate charge caused the 77th Ohio, the troops assigned to protect and support the battery, to retreat in haste leaving the guns and men exposed.[18] Whether true or not, Cushing said, "They ran without firing a shot."[19] They continued to fire without the luxury of protection until 10:00 a.m. when Sherman, acknowledging their exposed position, ordered them back to the Purdy Road, about one mile to the rear.[20] There the battery engaged the enemy for about two hours until their ammunition was exhausted. The unit then retired to replenish their supply of shot and canister and were not in action at Shiloh again.[21] If Cushing's recollection of the battle differs somewhat from the official version, it is understandable. Here was a raw recruit, within two weeks of his enlistment, thrown into the bloodiest battle thus far in the war. On June 18, 1898, the *Boston Post Express* printed a letter from Howard to his mother in which he describes the battle and tells of fighting for two and one-half days. He recalled fighting at the battery's first position for three hours, which may have been possible since the Confederates began their assault at 4:00 a.m. on the outermost pickets of the Union forces. However, he states they fought at the second position on the Purdy Road for an additional six hours. (Perhaps it just seemed that long to him.) Official reports tell of fighting at the second site for only two hours and then retiring from the field. Cushing, by implication, infers that the battery was engaged in the second day's fighting but official records belie this fact. He also recalls being given the order to march on Corinth with five days rations. This indicates this letter must have been written at the end of April when the slow advance toward that city began. A casual reading of this account would lead the reader to believe that the Union Army began its pursuit of the rebels immediately after the battle.[22]

After Shiloh, Major-General Henry Halleck arrived at Grant's headquarters and removed Grant from command. It was widely thought that Halleck, Grant's superior, was envious of Grant's successes at Forts Henry and Donelson. Shiloh gave Halleck an opportunity to brand the battle a Union failure, although, at worst, it was probably a stalemate. In the days to follow, Halleck's reputation as only an average field commander would manifest itself during the slow march on Corinth. Although the Battle of Shiloh had ended on April 7, the Federal army did not begin its march on Corinth until three weeks later on April 29. With an issue of five days rations, the army began its crawling advance to the south, Sherman's division guarding the right flank of the Union Forces. Halleck's timidity forced the troops to throw up defensive breastworks each night and the slightest encounter with enemy resistance caused the entire army to come to a halt. Finally, the Federals entered Corinth after taking almost one month to cover twenty-five miles only to find the city deserted by the enemy.

The battery report for June 1, 1862, does not record any events during the previous month. It merely states, "In the field near Corinth."[23] The unit was with Sherman's division but, if the fighting was sporadic and very light, it was probably not called into action. It was customary for artillery to be last in a column of advance following cavalry and infantry. It is inconceivable that, had they seen any action, however slight, the company commander would not have noted such activity in his official report.

On July 6, the battery moved to Moscow, Tennessee, arriving there on July 7. Encamped at Moscow until July 18, they then moved on successive marches to Collierville, White's Station, and thence to Memphis, arriving there on July 24.[24] On that same date Sherman was appointed Military Governor of Memphis and the battery was to camp there until some time in December, 1862. (Battery Reports for December, 1862 and January, 1863 are missing.) The report of February 1, 1863, states that the battery had been engaged at Chickasaw Bayou (or Bluffs), in an unsuccessful attempt to attack the city of Vicksburg from the north.[25] Chickasaw Bayou was an unlikely place to fight a battle. The Southern armies held the high ground as the Northerners tried to advance through the swampy land. Even when narrow, dry sandbars were found, advance was impossible because the area was covered by Confederate fire and abatis. The difficult terrain restricted the use of artillery but Cushing states he was present during the fighting.[26]

After Chickasaw Bayou the morale of the Union Army began to wane and the commanders knew a quick victory was necessary. Consequently, on January 1, 1863, Battery B was loaded on the steamer, *City of Memphis*, and proceeded down the Yazoo River and up the Mississippi River until the evening of January 8 when it transferred to the steamer *Henry Von Phiel*. Steaming up the White River and into the Arkansas River, the battery disembarked at a point about five miles below Fort Hindeman, also known as Post Arkansas. On January 10, the forces under the command of Major-General John McClernand marched toward the fort. Battery B took a position bearing on the rifle pits of the enemy and was in action for about two and one-half hours. At 4:30 p.m., Fort Hindeman surrendered.[27]

January 14 found the battery on the steamer *Chancellor*, and on the twenty-second they disembarked at Milliken's Bend on the Mississippi River. From there they marched to Young's Point on the west bank of the Mississippi northwest of the city of Vicksburg, Mississippi. The battery was now attached to the Second Division, commanded by Brigadier-General David Stuart, which was part of Sherman's Fifteenth Army Corps.[28] From January 26 through April 26 the battery was camped and inactive at Young's Point. On April 26 the battery was loaded on the steamer *J. H. Dickey* and transported to Milliken's Bend, Louisiana. On April 28, the officers, sixty-one enlisted men, four horses, six field pieces and twenty-four ammunition chests left Milliken's Bend under special orders from General Sherman.

Special Order No. 96, issued by Sherman, directed that "A combined gunboat and army expedition will be made up the Yazoo for the purpose of diverting the attention of the enemy from the movements now in progress below Vicksburg."[29] Section IV of this order directed Barrett's Battery, Battery B, to

be embarked from Milliken's Bend and to distribute one section of guns per boat and to barricade themselves on the forward deck with hay bales. The order further stated that there
was no intention of making an attack on the rebels at Hayne's
Bluff, but the commanders should be alert "to take advantage
of any opportunity afforded by events."[30] This squadron of
boats carried out the feint on the Confederate emplacements.[31]
The ruse worked and the Union Army crossed the Mississippi
south of Vicksburg and began a circuitous route overland,
advancing from the south and east toward the city.

Having returned to Milliken's Bend, Battery B set forth on
May 7, marching south along the west bank of the Mississippi to
Hard Times Landing, Louisiana, arriving there on May 11 and
on that same day crossing the river to Grand Gulf, Mississippi.
The next morning found them on a march to the northeast
toward Raymond, Mississippi. Leaving Raymond on the morning of the 16th, Battery B was engaged later in the day in the
Battle of Champions Hill.[32] Champions Hill was a small cres-
cent-shaped rise in the land, about seventy-five feet in eleva-
tion, on the plantation of one Sid Champion.[33] The battery was
located on the left of the line and did not see much action. In
the evening after the battle, Battery B was ordered to report to
the Tenth Division, Thirteenth Army Corps, Brigadier-General
A.J. Smith commanding.

On the following day the pursuit of the rebel forces began
anew, engaging them at the Battle of Big Black River. Battery B
did not participate but marched north of the battle site and
crossed the Big Black on hastily constructed pontoon bridges,
camping that night about two miles west of the stream. On the
morning of May 18, they commenced their march toward
Vicksburg and came within sight of the enemy defenses at
about 4:00 p.m. They fired a few rounds toward the city with
three of their guns and then ceased firing for the night. On the
nineteenth, the battery moved to a new position nearer the
rebel lines and at 11:00 a.m. commenced firing, "expending 200
rounds of fixed ammunition during the day."[34]

The next morning, one section of the battery was put in
position on the right of the Vicksburg Road. Firing was done at
intervals—ten minutes of firing, twenty minutes of rest—and

was directed at fortifications opposite the battery. During the fighting on this day Private Douglas Newell was killed and Private Henry Henroutin was wounded, but died from his wounds on May 26.[35] The next day the absent section returned and joined the battery in continued firing, the only casualties being three wounded horses.

Grant decided on an all-out attack to breech the defenses of the beleaguered city. To prepare for this attack, Battery B was ordered forward to a position within four hundred yards of the enemy works. Although the assault was doomed to failure, Battery B attempted to support the infantry advance, but such support was dictated by the position of friendly troops. Two such surges by Union troops were repulsed and the battery suffered one casualty, Private Frederick Thomsen, who was killed by a sharpshooter's bullet.[36] At this point, Grant, realizing that any more such attacks would result in needless bloodshed, decided to settle his army down to a siege of the surrounded city. Vicksburg, with the Union gunboats controlling the western approaches to the city and Grant's army in a semi-circle to the north, east and south was enclosed from all directions. The only problem presenting itself to Grant was an attack on the rear of his lines.

On June 3 Battery B embarked on the steamer *L.M. Kennett*, proceeded up the Yazoo River, and disembarked at Sataria, Mississippi. Marching with Mower's Brigade of the eighth Division, Sixteenth Army Corps, an advance was made toward Mechanicsburg, Mississippi. Rebel forces were driven through the town, thus diminishing the threat to the Union rear. Returning to Hayne's Bluff on June 7, the unit again embarked on June 9 aboard the steamer *Blackhawk* and proceeded to Young's Point, Louisiana. The Confederates, under the command of General David Taylor, were driven from their positions. Battery B fired 378 rounds of fixed ammunition during the fighting. Leaving the town of Richmond in flames, they returned to Young's Point on June 6. A significant event during the month of June was the loss of the battery commander, Captain Samuel Barrett. Barrett was promoted to the rank of Major and was relieved of command of the battery. The only remaining experienced officer was Second Lieutenant Israel

Rumsey who, because of his long tenure with the battery, was soon promoted to the rank of Captain.[37]

Battery B remained at Young's Point until the fall of Vicksburg on July 4, 1863, when Confederate General Pemberton surrendered the city to Grant. Amidst what was a joyful but subdued celebration, little did Howard Cushing know that his beloved brother, Alonzo, had been killed the previous day during the last-gasp charge of Pickett at Gettysburg. The day Vicksburg surrendered, the battery was loaded on the steamer *F. Ballet* and proceeded up the Mississippi River to Lake Providence, Louisiana, where enemy troops had been reported. They returned to Young's Point on July 7, having found "nothing worthy of note" at Lake Providence. On July 12 they crossed the Mississippi to Vicksburg and marched east to the Big Black River railroad bridge, arriving there on the twelfth and going into camp. On the twenty-second, the battery moved to Messinger's Ferry on the Big Black and again made camp. On the twenty-seventh, they were ordered to rejoin their original brigade (Second Brigade, Second Division, Fifteenth Army Corps) at Fox's Plantation, three miles from Messinger's Ferry.[38] Here the army set up summer camp to rest the troops from the arduous campaign. Many veterans, enlisted and commissioned alike, used this opportunity to take leave, most of them for twenty days.

Cushing did not take leave during this period, but began a letter writing effort to receive a commission as an officer in the Fourth United States Artillery, taking the place of his deceased brother. Cushing's letter of application to Secretary of War Stanton tells of his wartime experiences and leans heavily on the memory of Alonzo.[39] (See Appendix, Exhibit D.) Israel Rumsey, battery commander, also wrote a letter of recommendation, noting Cushing's knowledge of the drill of artillery and adding, "...his moral character is unexceptional." Rumsey, too, evokes the memory of Alonzo and intimates that the commissioning of Howard will do great honor to the deeds of Alonzo.[40] (See Appendix, Exhibit E.) Cushing's application was also endorsed by the original battery commander, Major Ezra Taylor, now Chief of Artillery, Fifteenth Army Corps.[41] (See Appendix, Exhibit F.) On August 21, 1863, President Abraham

Lincoln endorsed the application stating, "I know not whether this can be consistently done, but the case seems to be a meritorious one."[42] (See Appendix, Exhibit G.) However, given the oft-times strained relations between Lincoln and his Secretary of War, one wonders about the impact of the President's approval.

Secretary Stanton denied the original request citing policy forbidding promotion from a state militia directly into the regular army. On August 26, Howard's brother, Milton, then a Navy lieutenant stationed in Washington, wrote an impassioned letter to Stanton on Howard's behalf. He not only emphasized Alonzo's bravery but also of, "...his widowed and bereaved mother's sacrifice."[43] (See Appendix, Exhibit H.) By September 7, when it appeared no action was going to be taken, Milton wrote a letter to Assistant Secretary of the Navy Augustus Fox asking him to intercede with Stanton. Citing a method around the regulations, he suggested that Howard could be discharged from the state militia and then sworn into the regular army. Milton offers the example of an army clerk who formerly belonged to the Stutgis Rifles or, as he calls this group, 'McClellen's Body Guard,' who had been mustered out and then sworn in as a Second Lieutenant in the regular army.[44] (See Appendix, Exhibit I.) Assistant Secretary Fox then wrote to Colonel James Hardie, Acting Adjutant General of the Army, pleading Howard's case.[45] (See Appendix, Exhibit J.)

In the meantime, Cushing continued to serve with Battery B. On September 20, the battery left Fox's Plantation and marched to Big Black River Bridge, camping there until the twenty-seventh. On the twenty-eighth, the right section of guns embarked on the steamer *Atlantic* and the center and left sections departed on the steamer *Ohio Belle*, bound for Memphis, Tennessee.[46] The right section arrived at Memphis on October 3 and the remaining sections on October 5. Unfortunately, the transportation wagons and harness had been loaded on the steamer *Sam Gatz*, which sank when it hit a snag on September 28. Apparently the lost equipment was quickly replaced, for on October 8 they began a march to the east with the Third Brigade, Second Division, Fifteenth Army Corps. The march took them through the Tennessee towns of Germantown, Moscow,

LaGrange and Pochahontas before turning south to Corinth, Mississippi, where they camped from October 14 to 17th. Leaving Corinth, the march took them to Iuka, Mississippi on the eighteenth. The twentieth found them in Cherokee, Alabama. On the twenty-first, the Fifteenth Army Corps began a march on Tuscumbia, Alabama, only to find their advance blocked by the cavalry forces of Confederate General Nathan Bedford Forrest. Forrest was slowly driven back and although Battery B was placed in position, they took no part in any engagement. Finally, on the 27th the Federals reached Tuscumbia, driving the rebel army before them. On the twenty-eighth, Battery B marched back to their former camp at Cherokee and two days later moved to Chickasaw, Alabama, on the Tennessee River.[47]

November 2 they crossed the Tennessee River and marched to Gravelly Springs and reached Florence, Alabama, the next day. Successive marches during the next six days found them at Fayetteville, Tennessee on November 9. The next five days, November 10-14, were a series of marches that culminated in their arrival at Larkinsville, Alabama. On the fifteenth, they marched to Bellfonte, on the sixteenth to Stevenson, and arriving at Bridgeport, Alabama on the seventeenth.[48] The next day Howard Cushing received the news which he had been so eagerly awaiting since his first application to Secretary Stanton. Special Order No. 530 issued by the War Department arrived at Bridgeport ordering Private Howard Cushing to Washington, D.C. for discharge from the state militia in order to facilitate his commission in the regular army. Although his battery mates were to face the next great battle at Chattanooga, Cushing departed looking forward to this next challenge.

CHAPTER III

THE FOURTH U.S. ARTILLERY

Howard Cushing traveled to the Capitol as quickly as the transportation of the day and the disposition of the various armies would allow in order to assume his new rank. He was commissioned a Second Lieutenant in the Fourth United States Artillery on December 8, 1863. His letter of acceptance to Brigadier General Lorenzo Thomas, Adjutant General of the United States Army is dated December 8, 1863.[1] (See Appendix, Exhibit K.) He then proceeded to join his new assignment, Battery A of the same regiment, located at Brandy Station, Virginia.

His wish had come true, for he was assigned to the same unit as his departed brother, Alonzo. Upon reporting on December 18, he found himself the only officer present. The battery commander, Captain Charles Morgan, had been absent since August 5, 1863, acting as Assistant Inspector General of the Second Army Corps. Morgan had been assigned battery commander upon the death of Alonzo Cushing after the Battle of Gettysburg, and one month later he had been transferred to new duties. Second in command, First Lieutenant Rufus King, had been absent without leave since December 6, 1863, and the remaining officer assigned to the battery, Second Lieutenant Arthur Morris had been serving as Aide-de-Camp to his father, Brigadier General William Morris since January 17, 1862.[2] Although many of the non-commissioned officers came to like and respect Cushing, one can only imagine their feelings upon finding themselves commanded by a new Second Lieutenant just recently promoted from the rank of private. Fortunately for all concerned, Battery A did not figure in any immediate battle plans, perhaps because of the absence of any experienced officers, but more likely because armies traditionally went into winter camp.

In January 1864, the command remained the same except for King who is recorded as "Absent Sick" on January 28. This was changed to "Detached Service at Columbus, Ohio" on January 30. On January 26, Cushing left for fifteen days leave. Again, the battery was without a commissioned officer. Cushing returned on February 9 and assumed command, a post he would hold until April 4, 1864, when King returned.[3] Sometime after April 4 the battery moved to Stevensburg, Virginia, with Cushing now as second in command.

Attached to the Cavalry Corps commanded by Major General Phillip Sheridan, the battery next moved to Chesterville, Virginia, on May 3 and the next day to the site of the former battlefield at Chancellorsville. The following day they became engaged in the Battle of the Wilderness at Todd's Tavern. Todd's Tavern was located about one mile from the Wilderness at the intersection of the Brock and Orange Courthouse Roads, a strategic crossroads, the control of which was necessary to both sides for the free movement of troops and supplies. (Note: Many of the place names hereafter mentioned no longer exist on current maps. Fords and ferry crossings, boat landings, plantations and the like were named for families who lived at the location, geographical features or prominent structures. The reader, if interested, may follow army movements in the *Atlas to Accompany the Official Records of the Union and Confederate Armies, 1861-1865*, Government Printing Office, 1891-95.) There was to be sporadic but fierce fighting at Todd's Tavern for the next few days. On May 6, the battery marched to Piney Woods and engaged the rebel forces, only to return to

Todd's Tavern the next day for another engagement with the Confederate cavalry. On May 8, they returned to Piney Run and again met the enemy.[4]

On the evening of May 8, Sheridan and fellow General, George G. Meade, became embroiled in a severe disagreement concerning what Meade felt was Sheridan's error in not immediately moving his troops against Lee's retreating army at Spotsylvania. Meade had found Sheridan's troops sleeping beside the road near Todd's Tavern. Sheridan's intent was to rest his men after four days of movement and fighting but Meade vehemently disagreed with this decision. Expressing his anger to Grant, Meade relayed Sheridan's boast that, given the opportunity, he could "Knock Jeb Stuart out of action." Grant informed Meade to let Sheridan, "Start right out and do it."[5]

On May 10, Sheridan set out with ten thousand horsemen and thirty-two artillery pieces, including Battery A, in a column thirteen miles long to attack Richmond, Virginia.[6] His strategy was to draw the Confederate cavalry under J.E.B. Stuart away from the main body of Lee's army. Swinging his army to the northwest and then to the southwest, Sheridan moved his corps, the horses at a walk, slowly toward Richmond. This leisurely advance was intentional knowing that, once Stuart discovered his movements, he, Stuart, would have to gallop his horses to intercept the Union column. Sheridan wanted fresh horses for any meeting between the two armies.[7] His first objective was Beaver Dam Station, a major Confederate supply base. As the Union army approached, the depot guards set fire to 915,000 rations of meat and 504,000 rations of bread.[8] The guards fled and Battery A did not participate in any engagement here since there was very little resistance offered. On the next day the Battery did engage the enemy at Ground Squirrel Church, with the rebels quickly falling back.[9] On that same day Custer's brigade, along with two brigades of Merritt's division, tore up ten miles of railroad track to accompany the one hundred railway cars and two locomotives destroyed the previous day.[10] In addition they freed 378 Union soldiers captured at the Wilderness.

Stuart's dilemma was that he was unsure of Sheridan's objective—the rear of Lee's army or Richmond itself. He ordered a thousand men to come up on the rear of the Federal column to slow its advance and another twenty-five hundred men to stay with Lee. Taking the remainder, forty-five hundred men, he set out to intercept Sheridan. Arriving at Beaver Dam Station too late to save the supplies, his scouts soon informed him that the Union army was camped at Ground Squirrel Bridge. On May 11, Sheridan's army began to march down the Mountain Road toward Richmond. Stuart took the Telegraph Road, a parallel route, and, pressing his mounts to the fullest, hoped to stop the Federal advance where these two roads met to form the Brook Turnpike, the road to Richmond. Stuart arrived first and set up a defensive line north of the intersection at an abandoned stage station called Yellow Tavern. He also telegraphed Braxton Bragg, then commanding the defense of Richmond, warning him of the pending invasion.

At 11:00 a.m., Colonel Thomas Devin's brigade attacked the thin Confederate line only to be driven back by the 5th Virginia. In the meantime, Sheridan outflanked the Confederates and successfully cut off the Brook Turnpike, Stuart's only avenue of retreat. At 4:00 p.m., Sheridan ordered an all-out attack and Battery A, along with the rest of the Union artillery, poured round after round into the rebel lines. A prime objective was an already depleted Confederate battery which had been taking its toll of Union forces.[11] Stuart attempted to save this battery and the 1st Virginia met Custer's brigade in a hand-to-hand saber fight. The Federals were being driven back when a sharpshooter, forty-eight-year-old John Huff, snapped off a quick shot at a passing Confederate officer about thirty yards away. The man crumpled in the saddle and was led off the field. Huff did not know he had just mortally wounded J.E.B. Stuart and, in his absence, the rebel resistance faded away.[12] History would call this engagement the Battle of Yellow Tavern, but battery reports merely state, "On the 11th arrived at Richmond, Virginia. Engaged the enemy."[13] In these engagements, from Todd's Tavern to Yellow Tavern, Battery A lost two men to wounds— Privates Andrew Benvenute and Frank Coglan, both wounded at Todd's Tavern on May 7.[14]

Although Sheridan was convinced he could capture Richmond, he also knew he did not possess the force to hold the city indefinitely.[15] He decided to withdraw eastward to link up with

Benjamin Butler's Army of the James. At 11:00 p.m. on the evening of the 11th, the Federal forces began their retreat in a driving rainstorm. The road was peppered with land mines— artillery shells attached to trip wires strung across the road. After losing several men and horses to these missiles, Sheridan ordered rebel prisoners up to the front and had them crawl on their hands and knees ahead of the column, feeling for the wires.[16] Thus the army crept along and did not reach their first objective, Meadow Bridge, near Mechanicsville, Virginia, until daybreak. Intending to cross the Chickahominy River here, they found both the highway and railroad bridges partially destroyed by fire.[17] However, the heavy rains of the previous night had extinguished the flames before the bridges could be completely burned. Enough damage had been done that repairs had to be effected before the troops could safely cross. Across the river, Confederate cavalry, infantry and artillery were waiting for Sheridan to attempt a crossing. Under fire from the rebels and supported by artillery fire from the Union side of the river, engineers from Merritt's division repaired the bridges. In this engagement, Blacksmith Andrew Herlicker of Battery A was wounded, the last casualty of the war from Cushing's unit. In addition, four of the battery's horses were killed.[18]

Now attached to Gregg's cavalry, Battery A crossed the Chickahominy on May 13th and marched to Randall's Landing, arriving there on the fourteenth. Then began a series of marches seeking out the enemy or reacting to rumors of sightings of the foe. Leaving Randall's Landing on May 17, they marched to Baltimore Crossroads. On the twentieth, they reached the village of Cold Harbor, the site of a battle ten days later. May 22 found them marching almost due east to White House Landing. Still searching for the elusive rebel forces, successive marches found them at Ayletts, Concord Church, Polecat Creek, and on to the Panmunkey River. Finally, they engaged the enemy at Haws Shop. Battery reports place this engagement at Salem Church and Hanson's Store. The Battle of Haws Shop has also been called Salem Church and Enon Church.[19] Cushing locates this battle at Powhick Church for which no corroborating reference can be found.[20] The next few days found the battery on the march, again culminating in their arrival at White House

Landing on June 3. On the following day the battery was loaded onto the steamer *United States* and embarked for Washington, D.C. Arriving at Washington Arsenal on June 6, they marched the next day to Fort Totten located near Bladensburg, Maryland. Fort Totten was one of the many sites established in the defensive ring around Washington. Shortly thereafter they moved to Camp Barry which was not a large fortification but rather a battery placement outside a larger fort. They were to remain here until July of 1865.[21]

July 11, 1864, was the high water mark of Confederate General Jubal Early's raid on Washington. When he defeated Franz Sigel at Harper's Ferry and the Union army at Monocacy, the way to Washington was left unguarded. July 11 found Early's troops in the area of Silver Spring, Maryland, only a few miles from the capitol. The Confederates attacked Fort Stevens, the northernmost position in the defensive ring around Washington. It was here that President Lincoln was supposed to have stood on the parapet walls, exposing himself to enemy fire. Infantry skirmishing took place to the north of the fort on the 12th and in the afternoon of that day Early began to withdraw in the face of superior forces. A Cushing family biographer credits Battery A with manning 100-pound Parrot guns to aid in repulsing the Confederates' advance.[22] However, nothing in official records can substantiate this claim. It is highly unlikely that men so familiar with light artillery would be called on to man such heavy weapons.

On September 4, 1864, Cushing, along with a detachment of thirty-eight men, was ordered to a prisoner camp at Elmira, New York, an assignment that most probably went to the newest commissioned officer.[23] Officers senior to Cushing were certainly not interested in leaving the vicinity of Washington, the seat of power and influence. However, this was not to be an unpleasant assignment for Howard Cushing. It allowed him, until his recall some ten months later, to be near his hometown and his mother and sister. Although this assignment was not a difficult one, Cushing apparently had deep seated feelings toward Southerners in general and Confederate soldiers specifically. On one occasion, after one of the officers had been jeered and scoffed, Cushing had the prisoners assembled and remanded them in no uncertain terms:

See here you ---,---,---! I am just up from the front where I have been killing such infernal wretches as you are. I have met you in twenty battles. I never lost a gun to you. You never drove a battery I served with from its position. You are a crowd of insolent, cowardly scoundrels, and if I had command of this prison I would discipline you, or kill you, and I should much prefer to kill you. I have brought a battery of United States artillery to this pen, and if you give me occasion I will be glad to dam the river [pointing to the Chemung] with your worthless carcasses and silence your insolent tongues forever. I fully understand that you are presuming on your position as prisoners of war when you talk to me as you have; but [and here his hand shook warningly in the faces of the group], you have reached the end of your rope with me. I will kill the first man who again speaks insultingly to me while I am in this pen and I shall be here daily. Now, go to your quarters![24]

Of course, parts of Cushing's speech to the prisoners were clearly exaggerations, but the rebel inmates were in no position to challenge his claims. The battery returned to Washington in July 1865 after the prisoners had been paroled at the conclusion of the war. In September 1865, Cushing served as Acting Adjutant, Headquarters Battalion, Fourth Artillery, at Fort Washington, Maryland.[25] The battery, having been dismounted from the Cavalry Corps in July, was now stationed at Fort Whipple located just to the south of the Georgetown section of Washington, D.C. On November 4, 1865, an event occurred concerning Cushing's new commanding officer that was to alter the course of Howard Cushing's military career.

CHAPTER IV

CUSHING'S COURT MARTIAL

Captain Evan Thomas, a Brevet Major, was assigned command of Battery A, Fourth United States Artillery on November 11, 1864, by Special Order No. 397. At the time of his assignment he was serving as Aide to a Major General Thomas. Captain Thomas did not assume his new command until sometime in September of 1865, a full ten months after the special order had been issued and five months after the end of the war.[1] In the days ahead it became clear that Thomas was a hard drinking, temperamental man.

About noon on November 4, 1865, Mr. Walter Thompson was driving his wagon from Georgetown to the Virginia side of the Potomac River across what was called the Aqueduct Bridge. Two riders, later identified as Captain Evan Thomas and Acting Assistant Surgeon Henry Armstrong, passed Mr. Thompson while rapidly spurring their mounts. When the riders reached the middle of the bridge, Doctor Armstrong fell from his horse. Rising to his feet, he caught the bridle and attempted to remount. In so doing he fell over the saddle and onto the ground on the other side of his horse. Captain Thomas dismounted and attempted, with some difficulty, to assist his friend in remounting. Mr. Thompson, surveying this scene, inquired, "Captain, do you want any help there?"[2] At that point both men flew into a rage. Thomas demanded of Thompson did he know to whom he was speaking. Thomas then reached inside his coat, drew a revolver and fired at Thompson saying, "I'll blow your damn brains out!"[3] The bullet passed through the breast of Thompson's coat and exited, nicking the flesh of his right arm. The incident was witnessed by Private George Samisel of the 195th Pennsylvania Volunteers who later testified that he could not recognize either of the two officers involved.[4] However, both Samisel and Thompson could perceive and later testified that, clearly, both officers were intoxicated. After shooting Mr. Thompson, the men pulled their horses to the side of the bridge and allowed Mr. Thompson to pass. Remounting, the two horsemen galloped passed the Thompson wagon. Upon reaching the other side of the bridge, Armstrong again fell off his mount. This time there was room for Thompson to pass by. He proceeded and reported the incident to 'the fort.' Which fort is not known for there were three nearby the bridge — Forts Bennett, Corcoran, and Haggerty. Armstrong later testified that he and Thomas had been hoping to attempt the release of one Doctor Cuddy from arrest. Cuddy was the medical officer of Fort Wood.[5] Howard Cushing later stated that he had been made Officer of the Day by Captain Thomas when the latter left Fort Whipple. However, Thomas had retained the sash of Officer of the Day for his mission of effecting the release of Doctor Cuddy.[6] As a result of this altercation, a Court of Inquiry found, "Further proceedings are necessary."[7]

Four days later, November 8, 1865, Captain Evan Thomas, First Lieutenant Rufus King, and Second Lieutenant Howard Cushing, along with Alfred Newlin, late Captain of the 114th Pennsylvania Volunteers, went to Washington to attend the theater. Thomas, King and Cushing were transported to the city in an army ambulance driven by King's orderly, Private Henry Dutcher, while Newlin rode his own horse to meet the remaining officers. After the theater, the quartet retired to the Fountain Inn in Georgetown for a late meal and after-dinner drinks.

Upon exiting the inn, Newlin attempted to mount his horse on the sidewalk, the street being muddy. David Cunningham, a member of the Georgetown Metropolitan Police, arrested Newlin for drunk and disorderly conduct.[8] What precipitated this arrest is unknown except that it was illegal to have a horse on the sidewalk. Knowing Thomas' temperament, surely angry words were spoken. Cunningham took Newlin by the neck and proceeded to lead him toward the police station with the intent of locking him up for the night. This was too much for Thomas who followed the pair down the street, all the while berating the officer and calling him "a damned scoundrel, a damned coward, a damned puppy." This verbal abuse so outraged the policeman that when they reached the station house, Thomas was arrested for disorderly conduct.[9]

King and Cushing, having witnessed the proceedings, followed and attempted to persuade the jailer to release Thomas to them. Being aware of the problems Thomas faced due to the previous incident, King represented himself as the Provost Marshal of the district and requested that the Captain be given into his custody. Jeffrey Robinson, the jailer, refused this request knowing that a Provost Marshal from Fort Whipple had no authority in Georgetown. King then left and returned with a Negro boy carrying a bottle of liquor for Thomas and Newlin. Robinson ordered the bottle taken from the jail.

Cushing and King returned to the Fountain Inn to discuss, over drinks, what course of action they could take to release their commanding officer from jail. Whether their minds were befogged by alcohol or their mission so desperate, they foolishly decided to send Private Dutcher to Fort Whipple to order out a detail of men, under arms, to force Thomas' release. The inn's proprietor, George Tucker, overheard their plans and hastened to the police station to inform the officers there of Cushing and King's plans. Private Dutcher returned some time later with a detail of eight men, the only ones who would turn out in the middle of the night. Cushing returned to the fort and secured eight more men, placed them in the wagon and, mounting himself on a horse, returned to the bridge to join King and the other members of the detail.

The group then marched down the street to the jail and stood, fully armed with weapons loaded, in front of the building. King, now wearing the sash of Provost Marshal, and Cushing entered the station house and demanded Captain Thomas' release. King offered to sign a receipt for Thomas if the police would free him from jail. It is supposed by this time the police were becoming weary of King and Cushing's efforts. Cushing made matters worse by placing his elbows on the desk of Officer Robinson, positioned his face close to the policeman and saying, "You must give him up." Robinson left the desk with Cushing dogging his steps and insisting on the Captain's release. Cushing desisted when Robinson threatened him with arrest.

Finding the bluff of the use of troops ineffective, the men were ordered back to Fort Whipple. One of the solders was heard to say, "I wish to Christ they were all locked up so I could go home and go back to sleep." Cushing and King remained at the station house, Cushing sitting in a chair next to the stove and falling asleep.[10] King began to discuss the matter again, asking Robinson not to report his actions to the military authorities. Perhaps his mind was beginning to clear and he had begun to realize the illegality of his actions. He informed the policeman that, if reported, he possibly could be in a great deal of trouble from his superiors. Robinson advised King that he should have thought about the consequences of his actions before he took them. Cushing did not take part in this conversation. Upon awakening at daybreak, he left the station house.[11]

Within days, a Court of Inquiry was ordered held on December 4, 1865, into the matter of Thomas and the shooting incident and King and Cushing's attempt to free Thomas from jail. Cushing immediately took leave on November 13, 1865, for twenty days, returning one day prior to the meeting of the court. Courts of Inquiry were held to determine if there was enough evidence to charge the accused with a court martial offense, much like the Grand Jury of today. This proceeding could only be held at the request of the accused or by order of the President. Formerly, Courts of Inquiry could be formed at any time to determine if a full court martial should be held. However, the use of these Courts had been abused and subjected to influence for and against the accused. The system of army jurisprudence was then changed to allow only the accused or the President to call for the convening of such courts.[12]

At his Court of Inquiry, Cushing pled innocent, testifying he was only following the orders of a superior officer, a plea that exists today. King's testimony was basically unchanged except for one shocking statement. King avowed that his alleged purpose was to arrest stragglers stating, "Stragglers were in the habit of getting intoxicated."[13] 'Stragglers' was a Civil War term for Absent Without Leave (AWOL). It is fairly obvious that the four individuals in the second incident were not exactly sober themselves. At the end of testimony in Cushing's case, the Court found "Further proceedings were necessary."

On March 1, 1866, a General Court Martial was held in Washington in the matter concerning Howard Cushing's involvement in the attempt to free Captain Evan Thomas from jail. Cushing pled not guilty on all charges and specifications. (See Appendix, Exhibit L for a complete transcript of charges, specifications and findings of the court.) Cushing was represented by a civilian attorney, A.A. Hosmer, a lawyer practicing in Washington. The testimony given by the Georgetown police officers was essentially that given at the Court of Inquiry, *i.e.*, that Cushing, along with King, had attempted by various means to have Captain Thomas released from jail. It was testified again that Cushing had thrust his face into that of Officer Robinson demanding, "You must let him go," and "You know we can take him." Only when faced with arrest himself did Cushing cease these statements.

Cushing's defense, that he was obeying the orders of a superior officer, was countermanded by testimony of Lieutenant King. King stated under oath that he did not order Cushing to return to Fort Whipple for more men but rather asked Cushing if he were returning to the fort would he send more men. King testified that his statement was a request and not an order. Three enlisted men, Privates Charles Sharkey, Solomon Watson, and William Matfeldt, testified that Cushing roused them from bed stating that they were going to Georgetown and release Captain Thomas from jail by force. Sergeant William Nolan stated that at the station house Cushing had told him that he had protested these actions from the beginning. Sergeant

John Kintz testified that Cushing had told him, "(Bvt.) Major King's orders should be obeyed. Must be obeyed."

Attorney Hosmer attempted to refute the testimony of Privates Sharkey and Watson. Sergeant John Beale swore under oath he had heard Watson say, "He would shove the officers higher than a kite or shove them to hell if he could, no matter what he would have to say." Christian Maisack, formerly of Battery A but now a civilian, testified that he had heard Sharkey say, "He would shove the officers to hell to make up for old sores. He would state an untruth if he could not do it by fair means." However, since there were no corroborating witnesses to these statements, they were not considered as admissible evidence.[14]

As an interesting aside, shortly before the convening of the Court Martial Board, Howard's brother, Milton, wrote to their mother stating, "I see that Howard has been in some drunken scrape and is court-martialed. I hope he will not be dismissed, as I don't know what he will do. I will do no more on his behalf. And you had better let him understand that you will not."[15] What had happened between the two brothers to make Milton, who had staunchly supported Howard previously, abandon any support of Howard and request his mother to do the same? Was Milton so disgusted with his brother's actions that he even doubted that he could be a success in civilian life? Or perhaps it was the smear on the Cushing family name that so upset the older brother.

On March 14, 1866, the court rendered its decision. The panel found it impossible to believe that Cushing did not know of King's unlawful intentions in the release of Captain Thomas. Although the court alluded to Cushing's lack of experience and wisdom, he knew the "impropriety and illegality of his conduct." The sentence was ordered "To be suspended from rank and pay for the term of twelve months."[16] The sentence became effective on April 17, 1866, by Special Order No. 103, Adjutant General's Office, War Department.[17]

In retrospect, one wonders why Cushing and King formulated such a plan to effect the release of Captain Thomas. Both knew of their commanding officer's involvement in the shooting incident four days previous. They also were aware that a charge of drunk and disorderly on November 8 would not enhance any defense Thomas might offer on his behalf. Were their actions out of loyalty or were they out of fear of the Captain's temper? There is, however, another factor to be considered. These were men who had survived the bloodiest war in the nation's history. Through the course of that conflict the rights and needs of the civilian population had been superseded by the necessities of the military. Especially in the South, burning and looting had been tolerated and abuse of the civilian population was commonplace. It is possible that the mind-set of Thomas, King and Cushing toward civilian authority was still fixed in this wartime mentality. We will never know what prompted their actions or innermost thoughts, and all that has been offered as a reason for their deeds is merely speculation.

Officers serving terms such as those imposed on Cushing were left in limbo. For the length of their sentence they were no longer members of the army. They received no pay or emoluments, meaning rations or medical care. Their status on any regimental promotion lists was held in abeyance so that those with less experience moved ahead of them. As a matter of fact, the only mention of Cushing to be found in battery returns for the next twelve months is that of being on suspension for the term of his sentence. Since no personal records exist, one can only speculate. Most officers in this status simply returned home to wait out the time. Mary, being the loving mother she was, probably welcomed her son in her home despite Milton's admonition.

The next mention of Howard Cushing in official records is a letter addressed to President Andrew Johnson requesting that his sentence read "Suspended from pay and command" rather than "Suspended from rank and pay." He further states that Thomas was sentenced to "dismissal and hard labor for a period of two years" and King was sentenced "to be dismissed from the service." Although these sentences were later altered to be the same as Cushing's, he contended that his was the greater burden for a lesser offense.[18] (See Appendix, Exhibit M.) What probably precipitated this action was Captain Thomas' sentence being mitigated and Thomas being restored to battery command on January 1, 1867.[19] Cushing's request was denied in a letter from E.D. Townsend, Assistant Adjutant General, dated May 26, 1867.[20]

Cushing returned to duty on April 27, 1867, ten days after the expiration of his suspension. His lateness was excused by a Surgeon's Certificate of Disability. Cushing perhaps realized that his future military service with the Fourth Artillery was in jeopardy. Not only did he have a court martial offense on his official record but also his status as an officer had been lessened by his suspension in rank for one year. Cushing decided that a change of scenery was necessary.

CHAPTER V

EFFORTS TO TRANSFER

Without waiting for a reply to his plea addressed to President Andrew Johnson requesting the terms of his sentence by court martial be lessened, Cushing began to seek avenues of escape from the Fourth Artillery. The most difficult hurdle he encountered was the specific regulation concerning transfers. This regulation spelled out in very graphic terms the almost impossible task of an officer to transfer from one branch of the army to another:

Article VI Exchange or Transfer of Officers

par.30. The transfer of officers from one regiment or corps to another will be made only by the War Department, on the mutual application of the parties desiring the exchange.

par.31. An officer shall not be transferred from one regiment or corps to another with prejudice to the rank of any officer of the regiment or corps to which he is transferred.

par.32. Transfers will seldom be granted -- never except for cogent reasons.[1]

The army's reluctance to transfer experienced officers from one branch to another resulted in most officers spending their entire tenure in the same organization. Cushing's first task was to find a fellow officer eager to leave his present assignment and trade places with him. Seemingly, it didn't matter where he went as long as the new posting freed him from the stigma of his court martial offense. Most of the time such an exchange could be expedited by placing a notice in the *Army-Navy Journal*, a publication eagerly read by members of the armed forces. By whatever means, Cushing found his alter-ego in Second Lieutenant P. H. Ray of the Thirty-third Infantry with regimental headquarters in Atlanta, Georgia. On May 6, 1867, a request was made to the Adjutant General of the Army to approve the exchange of these two officers.[2] (See Appendix, Exhibit N.) On May 8 Captain Evan Thomas, Cushing's commanding officer, gave written approval to the transfer, although in lukewarm terms, stating that the transfer "be made if possible."[3] Colonel Edw. Canby, commanding the Fourth Regiment of Artillery, forwarded his endorsement the same day.[4] In a surprising move the next day, Cushing applied for a transfer to the Third Cavalry "...to fill an existing position."[5] On May 10, Thomas endorsed this second transfer, followed on May 15, by Canby's approval.[6]

Howard Cushing now had two transfers pending in the shuffle of army paperwork. Then, for some reason, he withdrew his application for transfer from the Fourth Artillery on May 22, 1867.[7] Whatever the reason for his request for withdrawal, it all became meaningless. On June 7, 1867, Colonel N. H. Ruger, commanding the Thirty-third Infantry, returned a curt reply of, "Transfer disapproved."[8] This was followed three days later by a disapproval from Lieutenant Colonel B.S. Roberts, commanding the Third Cavalry. Citing regulations, Roberts also noted that Captain Thomas did not seem earnest in his endorsement.[9] (See Appendix, Exhibit O.) The official denial came on June 27 and 28 when both transfers were disapproved by General Ulysses S. Grant.

Undaunted by these failures, Cushing forged ahead. Not content with previous denials, he searched for and found another officer willing to exchange places with him. Second

Lieutenant James Dixon, Third United States Cavalry, submitted on May 18, 1867, a request for transfer to the Fourth Artillery in an exchange with Second Lieutenant Howard Cushing of
that regiment. On the same date Cushing submitted a like request. In Dixon's favor was his service with the Second Connec-
ticut Artillery Volunteers in the past war.[10] On September 7,
1867, Special Orders No. 436, Item 8, directed that the transfers
of Cushing and Dixon were approved and that both officers
were to "...join their proper stations without delay."[11] However,
the term "without delay" would be a relative one for Cushing.
Travel to the Southwest in 1867 meant a long and arduous trek.
One could go by sea to the Gulf coast or travel overland via the
recently completed transcontinental railroad. Either route left a
long trip to join the Third Cavalry in New Mexico Territory.

The *Army-Navy Journal* of April 25, 1868, reported a detachment of two-hundred-fifty recruits for the Third Cavalry,
commanded by Second Lieutenant H. B. Cushing, left Carlisle
Barracks, Pennsylvania, bound for the Southwest.[12] To under-
take such a journey alone was most difficult but an individual
had the advantage of flexibility. Not so with two-hundred-fifty
recruits; to transport, feed, and keep together these inexperienced soldiers was a formidable task. Although details of this
cross-country trip are unavailable, Cushing and his small army
persevered. Upon his arrival at Fort Union, Cushing was sworn
in as a Second Lieutenant, Third Cavalry on July 21, 1868. This
was necessary because his former rank in the Fourth Artillery
was no longer valid. Upon dropping his right hand after taking
the oath he immediately raised it again to be commissioned as a
First Lieutenant in the same regiment.[13]

A careful search of regimental records sheds light on this
startling development. Troop F, the unit to which he was ul-
timately assigned, had several temporary commanders during
1868. Captain Richard Wall commanded the Troop until
September 20, 1868. On August 31, 1868, George McMullen
was promoted from First Lieutenant to Captain and assigned
command of Troop F. However, on the next day, September 1,
he tendered his resignation from the army and awaited a reply
at Cimmaron, New Mexico Territory. On September 21, 1868,
command of the Troop passed temporarily to First Lieutenant

Peter Vroom of Troop H. Since it would have been highly irregular for a Second Lieutenant to command a company on any but a temporary basis, Cushing had been commissioned a First Lieutenant and relieved Vroom of Troop F command on September 30, 1868.[14]

Although his service in the Civil War with Sheridan's Cavalry Corps may have given Howard Cushing some firsthand observation of cavalry tactics, he was by no means an experienced leader of mounted troops. It is questionable that any methods used in the previous war would prepare one to fight this new foe. Battles and/or skirmishes would no longer be fought by corps or divisions or brigades but rather by companies or troops or detachments of the same. Gone were the glory days of the grand charge, sabers flashing in the sun and attacking an enemy who used the same tactics as oneself. The Indians Cushing was to face fought their adversaries in a much different fashion. Sly and skillful warriors, the Indians of the Southwest, especially the Apache, were to prove to be the most fierce enemy the army had thus far faced. Fighting from cover and ambush, the Apache engaged the army on their own terms, choosing the place and time for battle. Indians, unlike the army, did not have an endless supply of reinforcements. Any Indian killed in battle could only be replaced by a succeeding generation, whereas the army had merely to request replacements from the nearest recruiting depot.

Two concepts were in vogue during this period—Manifest Destiny and Total War. Manifest Destiny was not an official doctrine but rather a phrase coined to justify the migration of eastern peoples to the unsettled lands of the West. In the beginning the West was Ohio and Kentucky, but it later encompassed all of any territory acquired by treaty or conquest. Americans, eager for a better life, felt it was their God-given right to occupy all lands now within the boundaries of the continental United States. Indeed, settlement was encouraged by the Homestead Act of 1862 which gave ownership of land to settlers who would occupy and improve their properties. Most of those involved gave no consideration to the Native Americans on whose lands they were to take ownership. Initially, the Apaches tolerated these intruders, their totals being small, but when the numbers of settlers began to swell, tribal leaders sensed the danger to their way of life. The Indians never understood the white man's passion for ownership of land, for to them the land and the benefits thereon belonged to all. The protection of these scattered groups of people fell to the widely spaced outposts of the army.

The second concept, Total War, was fashioned during the War of the Rebellion. Up to and including the beginning of that conflict, war was waged between gentlemen. There are many accounts of the kind of treatment of captured and wounded officers by their enemy counterparts. By and large, where possible, the civilian population was spared the agonies of warfare with, of course, the exception of the loss of loved ones. Many battles were fought over open ground, away from any concentration of hapless people. As the war ground on, southern cities and their factories of supply became targets of the Union Army. Sherman's destruction of Atlanta and his subsequent march to the sea and Phil Sheridan's raid through the Shenandoah Valley are prime examples of punishment of the civilian population for their support of a cause. In both of these instances homes and field crops were burned and supplies were pilfered for use by the invading forces leaving the affected people without any means of support. Grant's siege of Vicksburg, the Federal forces lobbing mortar shells and artillery rounds into the beleaguered city, forced the exhausted occupants, both civilian and military, to surrender. Total War now extended itself to the conflict with Native Americans in the belief that the extermination of these indigenous peoples was the sole answer to safe westward expansion. Sheridan's acknowledged statement, "The only good Indian I ever saw was dead," was indicative of this period of history. However taken in the spirit of the time, most Americans accepted these so-called doctrines.

Indians were portrayed by newspapers and pulp magazine writers of the period as bloodthirsty savages waiting to prey on helpless women and children, raping and pillaging without any respect for human dignity. Perhaps no race, until the emergence of the Nazi regime in the 1930s, was so despised by the American people. Policy concerning the treatment of Indians was formulated in the East by political appointees who had never seen an Apache. Left to the army was the enforcement of these sometimes misguided policies, at times a seemingly impossible task. Indians never accepted fully any rules that bound them to a certain parcel of land, having freely roamed for hundreds of years over territory now occupied by the white man. To the army was left the task of conquest, a formidable one to be sure. In the Southwest, from the conclusion of the Civil War to Geronimo's final surrender, the army waged war on the tribes of New Mexico and Arizona Territories. During this time new tactics had to be learned and the rules of warfare espoused by Clausewitz forgotten.

Who were these people, the Apache? The name Apache comes from the Zuni word "Apachu" meaning enemy. The Apaches never called themselves by this term but rather by their tribal names −N'de, Dine, Tinde, Inde and others, all meaning "The People."[15] They fed themselves with available vegetation or animals of the hunt. Their religion consisted of reverence toward the land and legends that explained the occurrence of natural events that modern man accepts with casual aplomb. On foot until the Spanish conquest, the Apache soon became a skilled horseman when these animals became available. Primarily a bow hunter, he quickly mastered firearms to his advantage although he never totally abandoned the weapon of his ancestors. For centuries he had freely roamed across what was to become the United States-Mexico border. This invisible line drawn in the sand and water held no real meaning for the Apache. They did begin to realize the impor-tance of this boundary when soldiers in pursuit stopped at the border, bound by treaty not to cross the line. Eventually troops in pursuit were permitted into Mexico, but for the most part the elusive Indians were able to slip away undetected. When chased by Bluecoats, war parties would break up into smaller groups and by circuitous routes rejoin below the border. Warfare and raiding for subsistence was a large part of Apache culture and the mere presence of Federal troops did not deter them from their centuries-old ways. Although it is true that some Apaches settled down on reservations set aside for them, there were elusive bands that refused to be conquered. To the army fell the

task of subduing these recalcitrant groups and bringing them
into the fold of peaceability.

Cushing inherited Troop F, hardly seasoned soldiers. Many
of the fifty-six privates were recruits who had accompanied him
from Carlisle Barracks. Those remaining were veterans of two
or more years' service, one dating back to the Civil War. A
significant fact in his favor was the abundance of non-commissioned officers, some of whom became his second-in-command
in the coming months.[16] Cushing was to be the only officer
present until Second Lieutenant Franklin Yeaton was assigned
to Troop F upon his graduation from West Point. The troop
commander, Captain McMullen, went home to Philadelphia on
sick leave, never to return. Second Lieutenant Scott Robinson
was sent on detached service on September 20, ten days prior to
Cushing's taking command. This situation may have made a
more timid officer reluctant in the field activities. However,
timidity had no part in Howard Cushing's make-up. He faced
every challenge with fearless, if not sometimes reckless, courage.

CHAPTER VI

WITH THE THIRD CAVALRY IN NEW MEXICO

At long last Howard Cushing had his own command, a circumstance that one year prior would have seemed only a pipedream given his status in his former regiment. However, ahead lay the task of molding into fighting condition a collection of inexperienced soldiers. Army procedures of the day did not include the basic training afforded to today's recruit. Enlistees of the nineteenth century were assembled at a recruiting depot and remained there until assigned to a regiment. Their stay at the depot may have been for a period of a few days to a month or more. During this cycle of service the men received uniforms and some very sketchy training in army procedures. When enough personnel had been assembled to meet the needs of a particular regiment, they were transported to their final destination. Contrary to the popular belief of today not every male person of the 1800s was adept at riding a horse or firing a weapon. These abilities had to be taught at the troop level under the charge of the troop commander or, more probably, by the non-commissioned officers. Many recruits were urban

residents who had no use for firearms or the need for eques-
trian skills. Others were immigrants who joined the army to
learn to speak and comprehend English. In actuality, an ideal
recruit would have been a lad from the farm. Since the population of the United States at this time was largely agrarian, those
young men growing up on the farm were expert in the very skills
that had to be taught to new soldiers. However, generally
speaking, this type of individual had no need to enlist for army
service. His basic needs were met by his everyday work, and
only those unhappy with the sometimes difficult life on the
home place left to find other avenues of income.

Thus, while veteran and recruit alike trained for battle, it is
plausible that they looked with askance at their new leader.
What sort of man was Howard Cushing? Was he the man to
lead them safely out of harm's way? John Bourke, who was
Cushing's second-in-command for many months describes him:

> He was about five feet seven in height, spare, sinewy,
> active as a cat; slightly stoop-shouldered, sandy complexioned,
> keen gray or bluish gray eyes which looked through you when
> he spoke and gave a slight hint of the determination, coolness
> and energy which...made his name famous all over the south-
> western border.[1]

Troop F did not have long to wait to see their first active
duty. Special Order No. 160, issued at Headquarters, District of
New Mexico, on October 20, 1868, ordered the troop to report
to Fort Bascom, New Mexico, for temporary field service in
what was to be called the Canadian River Expedition.[2] This
force, under the command of Major A. W. Evans, also included
Troops A, C, D, G, and I of the Third Cavalry and Companies F
and I of the Thirty-seventh Infantry.[3] In this circumstance
Cushing was fortunate. He and his inexperienced troops would
not be operating alone but rather with others and led by an
veteran officer in Major Evans. Troop F consisted of, in addition to Cushing, two sergeants, seven corporals, one bugler, two
blacksmiths, one artificer and forty privates. Ten enlisted men
were on detached service and two were listed as sick.[4] The
number of enlisted men varied. Those on detached service, sick,

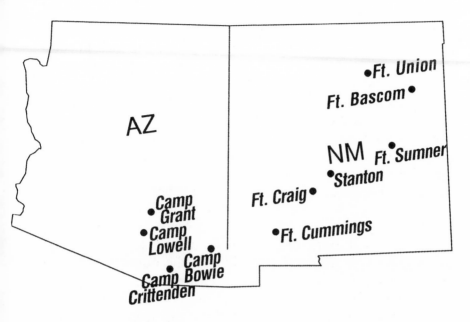

Forts and Camps in the New Mexico and Arizona Territories.

or in confinement swelled or lessened the ranks. Leaving Fort Stanton on October 24, 1868, and arriving at Fort Bascom on October 31, Troop F, as part of the forenamed expedition, departed on November 15 and marched to Monument Creek, Texas. Arriving at that place on December 15, they established a supply camp.[5] After the installation of this base camp, the expedition went on scout after hostile Indians. On December 25, 1868, they attacked and destroyed a Comanche village of "sixty lodges, a large quantity of provisions, implements of war and other property of great value to the Indians."[6] Regimental records indicate this fight to be on the Salt Fork of Elm Creek, Indian Territory, now the State of Oklahoma.[7] *The Chronological List of Actions With Indians, Etc...* places this action on Elm Creek (Salt Fork of), Indian Territory.[8] (It should be noted that on occasion Regimental and/or Troop records and the *Chronological List...* do not compare favorably. The author has attempted to correlate any events in a meaningful manner.) After only one conflict with Indians of the region, the troops moved to a point on the Washita River about fifteen miles above Fort Cobb, Indian Territory. The Indians had scattered, no doubt in response to the expedition's raid but also in reaction to George Custer's foray against Black Kettle's village on the same Washita River in late November of 1868.

On January 3, 1869, the expedition departed from the Washita and returned to the supply camp on Monument Creek, arriving on January 14. On January 28, the entire group began to wend its way back to New Mexico. On February 13, while at Fort Bascom, orders came dismantling the expedition and ordering the various troops to return to their original stations. On February 14, Troop F departed for Fort Stanton, traveling via Fort Sumner, and arriving at their home post on February 28, 1869.[9] It is doubtful that an expedition of this size and scope could be deemed successful considering the number of troops and the time and distance involved. However, any victory over hostile Indians was always judged a major accomplishment.

During the month of March 1869, the troop performed garrison and escort duty, probably the most boring segment of a soldier's life. Stable call, drill, and escorting wagon trains could not replace the euphoria of field service. On April 9, this monotony was broken when, in conjunction with Troops A and H, Third Cavalry and Company I, 37th Infantry, Troop F left Fort Stanton to scout for hostile Indians as part of the Apache Indian Expedition. They scouted through the Sacramento Mountains to the Rio Peñasco and on to the Rio Azuel where a supply camp was established. Leaving the Rio Azuel, the expedition then scouted the Guadalupe Mountains, returning to the supply camp on April 28. The next day the troops set out for the Rio Peñasco, arriving there on April 30.[10] *The Chronological List of Actions...* lists a fight with Indians at Sangre Canyon, New Mexico, on April 22, 1869, with a report of five Indians wounded.[11] The company muster report for this same period makes no mention of this engagement. For whatever reason, it is doubtful that Troop F took part in this fight. One cannot imagine a man such as Cushing missing an opportunity to include himself and his men in an official report concerning any Indian fight. This would be akin to the British Army tradition of being "mentioned in the dispatches."

Leaving the Rio Peñasco, the expedition resumed its march covering a distance of one-hundred and eighty-one miles through the Sacramento Mountains via Willow Springs, Ojo de Cuero, Alamo, LaLuel and Canyon Del Para to the Bacaez Ranch, seven miles from Tularosa, arriving on May 10, 1868. After resting there, Troop F returned to Fort Stanton on May 15, 1869.[12]

From May 15 to July 24, the troop remained at Fort Stanton performing garrison duties. This tedium was broken when, on July 25, the troop left for a scout beginning in the Sacramento Mountains. After marching one-hundred-fifty miles, they camped on the Sacramento River. On August 1, they resumed their march to Fort Bliss, Texas, via Isleta, Texas. On August 15, during their return to Fort Stanton, Troop F attacked an Apache village near San Augustine, New Mexico, capturing their riding animals and provisions. This action was commanded by Captain Frank Stanwood of Troop H, with Cushing and Troop F acting in concert. The troop returned to Fort Stanton on August 22, 1869, having marched a distance of 498 miles.[13]

From the date of their return until early November, the troop remained at Fort Stanton. On October 6, Cushing received assistance in command by the arrival of Second Lieutenant Franklin Yeaton, recently assigned upon his graduation from the United States Military Academy at West Point, New York.[14] After receiving a report of cattle stolen from Carey's Ranch on the Rio Hondo, the troop set out to recover the stock. On November 18, after a pursuit of two hundred miles, they overtook the Indians and the stolen stock in a canyon on the north side of the Guadalupe Mountains. During this encounter, they recovered all the stock not consumed by the Indians, along with thirty Indian horses and mules. Loss to the troop was one corporal and one private, both severely wounded. Cushing and his men returned to Fort Stanton via Rio Pecos and Rio Hondo on November 30, 1869.[15] Ordered out on scout, the troop left Fort Stanton on December 10, 1869. After a march of two-hundred and three miles, they engaged hostile Indians at the head of Canyon Sanquinara in the Guadalupe Mountains on December 25, 1869. Troop F burned the *rancheria*, destroyed the winter provisions, and captured a large number of riding animals. During the fighting, Yeaton was severely wounded through the wrist and hand.[16] By today's standards this wound would not be considered serious. However, given the caliber and relatively slow muzzle velocity of the weapons of the period, there was probably much damage to muscle tissue. Cushing, enraged over the wounding of his fellow officer, resolved to fight these Indians again. Fashioning a crude travois for Yeaton, the troop marched through heavy snow to a sheltered place near the Rio Peñasco. Leaving a guard for Yeaton and the supplies, Cushing took the freshest men and mounts and set out after the hostile Indians again. He had guessed correctly that the Indians had assumed they had escaped and would be somewhere ahead mourning their dead. After a march of one-hundred thirty miles, at dawn he attacked the remainder of the Indians in a canyon on the south side of the Guadalupe Mountains near the head of Delaware Creek. The Indians fled from this unexpected attack leaving behind all their beef cattle and belongings.[17] Little did Howard Cushing know that in Arizona an Apache, upon learning of this attack, vowed to atone for this assault on grieving people.[18]

The troop returned to Fort Stanton on January 6, 1870, by way of Rios Pecos, Felix, Peñasco and Hondo. Remaining at Fort Stanton until February 17, the troop departed from that place en route to a new station at Camp Lowell, Tucson, Arizona Territory. At Fort Craig, New Mexico, on February 26, Second Lieutenant John Bourke replaced Yeaton as Cushing's second-in-command.[19] Marching via *Jordada del Muerto*, (possibly very near to the World War II Trinity Site), they crossed the Rio Grande at an abandoned army post, Fort McRae, near present day Truth or Consequences, New Mexico.[20] Company muster reports do not mention this crossing but place the next point of the march at Fort Seldon, located seventeen miles north of Las Cruces, New Mexico. From there they marched to Fort Cummings, just north of Deming, New Mexico and from there to Camp Bowie, Arizona Territory.[21] Leaving Camp Bowie behind, they reached their destination, Camp Lowell, located on the outskirts of the village of Tucson, Arizona Territory, on March 10, 1870. Two days later orders were received for Troop F to proceed to Camp Grant, Arizona Territory, some sixty miles north of Tucson. After some delay, Troop F took station at Camp Grant on April 18, 1870.[22] Bourke described Camp Grant. "It was recognized from the tidewaters of the Hudson to those of the Columbia as the most thoroughly Godforsaken post of all those supposed to be included in the annual Congressional appropriations."[23] Located at the confluence of the Rio San Pedro and the Aravaipa Creek, Camp Grant was a most unhealthy place. Fever and ague were common and, although these were popular names for these maladies, the illness was probably malaria. It may sound strange to think of malaria in arid Arizona, but it must be remembered that a century ago, prior to the influx of large numbers of people, many rivers and streams ran with water in all but the driest of seasons. It was desirable to locate remote army posts near water for obvious reasons but the unwanted side effect was malaria. The cause of the high fevers was unknown at that time, but it was recognized that moving those afflicted to higher ground away from the camps alleviated the symptoms.

On April 25, 1870, Troop F was ordered to scout along the Rio San Pedro to the Pinal Mountains. After scouting without success through the Pinal Mountains, the troop returned to Camp Grant on May 7 having marched a distance of one-hundred seventy-six miles.[24] Counter to any perceptions Hollywood may present, not all scouts or patrols were successful. Many were exercises in a show of force for, although the troops did not discover Indians, the Indians were aware of the army's presence.

At the end of May, 1870, Cushing and eleven of his men arrived in Tucson after escorting a wagon train from Camp Grant. While there, they received word of an attack on a wagon train between Tucson and Camp Grant. The detachment from Troop F, bolstered by fourteen men of Troop B, Third Cavalry, commanded by Second Lieutenant A.S. Smith, who happened to be in Tucson at the time, set out for Camp Grant. Their first concern was the safety of the civilians on the wagon train. Upon reaching the point of the attack, they found the citizen's trail leading toward Camp Grant. Simultaneously, they discovered a strong Indian trail to the northeast. Reporting to Camp Grant, they drew rations and increased their numbers with nine more

enlisted men from Troop F, plus thirty enlisted men from
Troop K, First Cavalry. Also with this force was Manuel Duran,
an experienced guide. Setting out after the raiders, they trailed
them to a small stream in the Apache Mountains.[25] One factor
in Cushing's favor was that a case of patent medicine was part
of the wagon train's cargo. Such nostrums were largely alcohol
in content. The Indians had been partaking of the loot, leaving
many incapacitated.[26] On June 6, 1870, the troops attacked the
Apaches, killing thirty and scattering the remainder.[27] It is
interesting to note that Cushing had wanted to attack the hostiles immediately but Duran had advised against it. Putting his
men into position according to the scout's advice, they waited
until first light to attack.[28] The troops returned to Camp Grant
having marched three-hundred thirty miles in their pursuit of
the Indians.

The troop remained at Camp Grant until July 22 when it left
the post on a scout after Indians who had attacked the Gatchell
and Curtis wagon train on the road between Tucson and
Florence, Arizona Territory.[29] After marching via the Rio San
Pedro and the Rio Gila they next moved to the Pinal Mountains
and there, on Pinto Creek, they attacked and destroyed Indian
cornfields and a *rancheria* of eighteen lodges.[30] Cushing's military career almost came to an end from an unexpected source
as the troop bivouacked next to a small stream near the town of
Globe, Arizona Territory. After unloading the pack animals,
Cushing noted formidable clouds approaching over the mountain tops. Quickly, he gave orders to move the supplies and
bedding to higher ground. This task was nearly accomplished
when, with no warning but sound, a wall of water rushed
through the narrow canyon. The flash flood completely covered
that portion of land where the troops would have camped for
the night. Cushing was swept away by the torrent and would
surely have drowned if not for the efforts of Sergeant John
Warfield and Private Daniel Miller, who pulled him from the
raging waters. This incident caused a twenty-four-hour delay to
allow for the drying out of sodden food, especially the
hardtack.[31]

Departing from this place of misfortune they marched to
the north slope of the Apache Mountains where, at Skirmish

Canyon, they came upon another *rancheria* and cornfields. Their approach had been discovered by Indian lookouts. Since there was no chance of surprise, the two sides exchanged gunfire and the Apaches fled. After destroying the *rancheria* and cornfields, they captured two Indian women who agreed to lead them to another Indian camp. Upon approaching the second site, the troops found the Indians concealed on the hillsides. The soldiers could do no more than fire randomly at their tormentors hidden behind rocks and trees. After the Indians faded into the mountains, the troops destroyed thirteen lodges along with all of the Indians' belongings.[32]

Returning to Camp Grant on August 6, 1870, the troop remained in place until August 26. On that day Special Order No. 74 was issued at Camp Grant as were Special Instructions from Department Headquarters.

Headquarters, Department of Arizona
Prescott, August 9, 1870

Lt. H.B. Cushing
3rd U.S. Cavalry
    (Through C.O., Camp Grant, A.T.)
    Lieutenant:

Upon being relieved from duty at Camp Grant, A.T., you will proceed without delay to Tucson, A.T. Upon arrival there you will seek an interview with his Excy. Gov. Safford, and obtain from him and others all the information you may think necessary in regard to the recent outrages, committed by Indians in that vicinity and the adjoining region with the view of enabling you to act promptly and understandingly. The Department Commander directs that you use every effort in your power to rid that section of Indians that infest it, and to this end you will keep your command habitually in action, scouting the country and particularly that portion west of the San Pedro River.

"H" Company of cavalry from "Camp Bowie" has been directed to be kept in the field, scouting the country east of the San

Cushing

Pedro River, and it and your command should endeavor to act in concert, and should, if the occasion arises, act in conjunction.

Should Gov. Safford be able to organize volunteers and should they feel disposed to act in concert, in conjunction with other regular forces, you are authorized to furnish them with Government rations and other A.C.S. at Tucson, or Crittenden will furnish them upon Ration Returns approved by yourself. You will move as unencumbered with baggage of every kind as possible, and draw your supplies from Tucson or Crittenden as you may think best, and this letter of instructions will authorize you to call upon all officers of the Quartermaster's Department to extend to you all the facilities you may desire, including competent guides and a reasonable number of packers.

You will furnish these Headquarters with weekly reports of your operation and you will continue your scouting until further orders, and the Department Commander hopes and trusts with results commensurate with your exertions.

E. W. Stone
1st Lt., U.S. Army
Act. Asst. Adjt. Gen.[33]

Troop F, Third Cavalry, was to become a 'flying squad,' able to operate independently of other commands. Orders in hand, Cushing and his men set out immediately for Tucson, arriving there on August 28, 1870.[34]

Lieutenant Alonzo Cushing, USA
Killed at Gettysburg

Photo Courtesy of Waukesha County Museum

Howard B. Cushing in uniform of
First Illinois Light Artillery

Photo Courtesy of Waukesha County Museum

Lieutenant William B. Cushing, USN

Photo Courtesy of Waukesha County Museum

Lieutenant Milton Cushing, USN

Photo Courtesy of Waukesha County Museum

Final resting place of Howard B. Cushing
at the Presidio in San Francisco. Note the
error on the inscription. The "F" is not part
of his name, but rather his troop designation.

Photo Courtesy of Conrad McCormick

Monument to the Cushing Brothers
Fredonia, New York

Photo Courtesy of the D. R. Barker Library
Fredonia, New York

Inscription to Howard B. Cushing
on the Cushing Monument,
Fredonia, New York

Photo Courtesy of D. R. Barker Library
Fredonia, New York

Cushing Monument Dedication
May 31, 1915, Cushing Park
Delafield, Wisconsin

Photo Courtesy of Waukesha County Museum

CHAPTER VII

WITH THE THIRD CAVALRY IN ARIZONA

Upon their arrival in Tucson, Troop F did not avail themselves of the normal, although crude, comforts of Camp Lowell. The post was located on the eastern edge of the town with few permanent buildings. They set up their own camp in what tents were available outside the Quartermaster's corral.[1] The corral was not inside the confines of the camp itself, but located next to the Quartermaster Depot which was in a rented building in the town proper. The Post Hospital was likewise in leased quarters. Since he was to operate unencumbered, Cushing probably did not want his men to fall even remotely under the influence of another officer, especially the Post Commander. If he had located within the boundaries of the established camp, there was always the possibility that his men, on idle days, could be assigned to menial duties in the camp. A perusal of Camp Lowell records reveals occasional conflicts between the Post Commander and the Quartermaster concerning duty men and escorts. Troop F made themselves as comfortable as possible, pitching tents and constructing ramadas, crude brush covered awnings, to protect themselves from the scorching summer sun. Cushing and Bourke availed themselves of rented rooms in the town as was the custom for most officers.[2]

Although no official written record exists, Cushing in all probability followed orders and met with Governor Safford. Eager to start on his new assignment, Cushing wasted no time in putting his troops into motion. Two days after his arrival in Tucson, they set out on a scout through southeastern Arizona. Marching to the east they reached Tres Alamos on the Rio San Pedro the next day. Although a popular cavalry saying was "Forty miles a day on beans and hay," in most cases this was not an accurate assessment. In effect, most scout camps were located near or at available sources of water for men and animals. Of course, the Apache was aware of this tactic, for he himself used the same methods in his rovings and, more importantly, in his escape from Federal troops. Thus a move from water source to water source would not necessarily entail the distance troopers claimed in their saying. Forty miles each day would require strenuous riding and inflict great hardship on men and animals alike. To complicate matters, the Apache, in order to retard pursuit, oftentimes polluted water holes with dead animals, thereby making the water unfit to drink.[3] Water, being essential to life, was a necessary consideration in choosing overnight or longer camps. No soldier wanted to make 'dry camp' although this was necessary in extreme situations.

Setting out from Tres Alamos, the troop scouted the mountains to the east, south and southeast of Tucson with no success at locating hostile Indians.[4] On this scout the troops were accompanied by Governor Safford along with an unknown number of Mexican volunteers. Bourke recalled an interesting incident during this scout. Camping near the present town of Tombstone, the leaders were informed by Victor Ruiz, a Mexican guide, that he was interested in testing the memory of his grandfather concerning the location of a silver mine supposed to be located nearby. The riches of Spain intrigued the entire party. In a short time the old mine shaft was located and ore samples were extracted. However, their dreams of wealth were crushed when an assay proved any mining venture useless. The value of the ore was far less than the cost of reducing it to silver.[5] The troop returned to Tucson on September 24, having marched 473 miles.[6] As can be determined, the march averaged about nineteen miles per day.

Contrary to orders, Cushing's troops were not constantly on the move. Aimless wanderings would not have been in any way productive. Men and horses had to be rested and resupplied. Camps on scouts required sentries, leaving men at times without adequate rest; thus a pause from the rigors of scouting was necessary for both men and horses. Upon returning from his first scout under the new orders, Cushing rested his men for six days before setting out again. Marching only ten miles they came upon fresh Indian signs and began to trail the hostiles. Following this sign for five days they came upon the Indians at the head of Deer Creek in the Pinaleno Mountains. Quickly they attacked the Indian camp, killing two and probably wounding more. The troop did not escape unscathed. Private Andrew Smith was slightly wounded in the right side and Private Lewis Shire severely in the left leg.[7] Shire's condition was serious. The bullet had entered his left kneecap and ranged down his lower leg coming to rest near the ankle. The wound was not bleeding externally but was surely hemorrhaging internally. Shire was in great pain and there was no medical person accompanying the troop to offer succor. Recognizing Shire's pain and realizing the distance they were from assistance, Cushing, Bourke and Sergeant John Warfield drew to one side away from the camp-fires to discuss their next move in regard to Shire's relief. The nearest medical facility was at Camp Grant and it was determined to move Shire there the next day despite the fact that there was at the time no medical officer in attendance at the post.

At 4:00 a.m. the following morning the move began. Placing the wounded man on horseback with fellow troopers supporting him on both sides, they began the painful descent off the mountain. Each jolting step of the horse meant pain for the private, and their path down the slope was slow and tortuous. Upon reaching level ground, the party rested while Bourke and Private Thomas Harrington set out at a gallop for Camp Grant to procure an ambulance. A courier was sent to Camp Lowell in Tucson to summon and escort Acting Assistant Surgeon Henry

Durant, the closest doctor available, to come to Shire's aid. At Camp Grant preparations were made for the inevitable amputation.[8] Cushing did not accompany the detachment with Shire but continued scouting with the remainder of the troop. They rode through the now familiar Pinal and Apache Mountains, returning to Tucson on November 21 via the Rios Gila and Bonita.[9]

On December 5, 1870, the troop set out again marching north past the Santa Catalina Mountains to the Rio San Pedro. At Mount Turnbull they attacked an Indian rancheria, destroying the Indian property and scattering the natives through the hills. Destroying winter stores was considered second only to the actual killing of Indians in effectiveness. From Mount Turnbull they moved to Camp Goodwin and from there to Tucson, arriving on December 22, 1870.[10] Two days later they hurriedly mounted again after receiving a report of a trail left by Indians who had allegedly made off with a herd of cattle. Following this trial for about fifteen miles they soon came upon Mexicans, not Indians, who had been searching for their missing stock. Satisfied that these men were the rightful owners of the recovered cattle, Troop F returned to Tucson the same day.[11] This unproductive scout was indicative of the uneasiness of the populace at any hint of the proximity of Apaches. Any new trail through the yellow grass or the track of unshod horses through the sand gave cause for great alarm.

After celebrating Christmas in camp, the troop quickly mounted and departed riding northwest on December 27. Indians had attacked a wagon train owned by Tucson merchants Pinkney Tully and Estavan Ochoa. Following the trail until they became convinced that a large number of cavalry were on the same track, they abandoned the chase. Camping on the north side of the Santa Catalina Mountains on December 31, they returned to Tucson the next day.[12]

More than a month passed with no activity against the Apaches. However, on February 7, the Indians rustled cattle very near to the town. The Apaches had a tremendous head start and Troop F hastily took pursuit, picking up the trail on the Rillito Creek. Tracking the raiders through the Santa Catalina Mountains, the trail led them to the Sierra Galiuro. Here they were fired upon by a small party of Aravaipa Apaches who scattered after the first volley. They believed this was the rear guard of a larger band. Pushing on through a heavy mountain snowstorm, the troop attacked a large *rancheria* on February 13, destroying provisions and other Indian property, and recovering the stolen cattle, except for those consumed by the tribe. Leaving a small guard with the herd, Cushing led his men to the Aravaipa Mountains. There, on the next day, they discovered and destroyed another *rancheria* as the Indians fled to the hills. Returning to Tucson on February 18, from this most successful scout, Cushing, flushed with success, found that change had come to the command of Troop F.[13]

On December 15, 1870, General Order No. 126, issued by the Adjutant General's Office, ordered Captain Alexander Moore to return to active service. The reorganization of the army in 1868 left a surplus of officers with no assignment and these individuals were a sort of reserve until the need for them arose. Moore, a native of Ireland, had served in the Civil War, initially as an officer in the 13th Wisconsin Infantry and later as an aide to Generals Hooker and Sickles. Mustered out in 1866 he was commissioned as a captain in the 38th Infantry in 1867 serving in New Mexico as commandant of Fort Cummings. On November 11, 1869, he was left unassigned through the process of reorganization.[14] Infantry regiments had been reduced to twenty-five in number, leaving many officers without a posting. Relinquishing command of Troop F to Moore should not have come as a surprise to Cushing since General Order No. 365, issued by the Adjutant General on December 17, 1870, assigned Moore to the command of the troop.[15] Moore had accompanied recruits to the southwest prior to his arrival in Tucson.[16]

One of Moore's first actions as troop commander was to move his charge from the town of Tucson to a camp some miles away on the Rillito Creek. It is believed by some students of western military history that Cushing initiated this move soon after the troop's arrival in Tucson. However, it was not until Moore's assumption of command that official correspondence began to be dated "Camp on the Rieta [sic Rillito] near Tucson." Prior to this time, correspondence and official reports were dated merely "Tucson." The reasons for this move may have been twofold. Moore was probably attempting to exert total influence over his new command which had been led by Cushing for almost three years. Also, such a move would concentrate all his men in a single place, ready for action, away from the temptations of the town. Of Cushing's reaction to these changes we know little. Surely there must have been some resentment on his part upon being relieved of command by an infantry officer inexperienced in the tactics of fighting Indians. One is left to ponder why Cushing was not promoted to the rank of captain and allowed to continue his assigned task. In December 1869, Cushing had been recommended for the Brevet rank of captain for his actions .against the Indians of New Mexico. Brevets were highly prized by officers and had a significant influence on their careers. However, the request by General Schofield, commander of the Department of the Missouri, was denied by General Grant on the basis that "The brevet system has been so abused that I am disinclined to recommend any more."[17] So Cushing remained a lieutenant, and his position as troop commandant was taken from him by Moore's appointment. Moore officially took command of the troop on February 11, 1871, while the troop was in the field on scout.[18]

The troop remained in camp 'in the field' until March 12, when it left on scout seeking hostile Indians. They marched north via the Tortillita Mountains, crossed the Rio Gila and reached Camp McDowell outside present day Phoenix on March 29. Departing from Camp McDowell they next moved to the Sierra Ancha where, on April 4, they attacked and destroyed a *rancheria* with all its contents, killing one Indian.[19] Continuing their search into the Apache Mountains, the troop, on April 11, laid waste to another *rancheria*, killing four, capturing two, and destroying the Indians' entire stock of supplies.[20] The next day, on the south slope of the same mountains, another *rancheria* was discovered and attacked. As a result of this fight, twenty-four Indians were killed and a large number wounded. As before, supplies vital to the tribe were destroyed. Heading south, the troop marched to their campsite outside Tucson, arriving on April 17, 1871.[21]

The three preceding Indian fights present somewhat of a dilemma for the researcher. Muster reports and regimental returns indicate that Alexander Moore was in command of the troop during this time. However, the *Chronological List of Actions...* credits these fights to Cushing. Did Moore allow Cushing to direct the troop in the absence of his experience in Indian fighting tactics? Or was Moore exhibiting the same failure of leadership with which General George Crook was later to accuse him of and bring court-martial charges to bear for an incident on the Powder River in Wyoming in 1876?[22] The answer might lie in the required reports the troop commander was to submit on a weekly basis to the District of Arizona Headquarters in Prescott. Unfortunately, these reports do not exist in the National Archives. Records of "Letters Received" by the Department of Arizona are not to be found for the years 1870 to 1880, although the Register of Letters exists beginning again in 1877.[23] The puzzle goes unanswered, and one can only credit Cushing's leadership in these three actions.

On April 18, the troop left their camp on the Rillito and marched eastward across the Rincon Mountains to the San Pedro River, probably near the site of the present day Redington Ranch. Returning to camp on April 22, the troop was idle until April 27 when Cushing, with a small detachment of men, went on a scout southward to the Mexico line.[24]

CHAPTER VIII

CUSHING'S LAST SCOUT

Special Order No. 5, issued by Captain Alexander Moore on April 26, 1871, ordered First Lieutenant Howard Cushing to take a detachment of men from Troop F, Third United States Cavalry, to scout the Sonoita and Santa Cruz valleys and the southern portion of the same along the United States-Mexico border.[1] (Author's Note: Much of what follows, except where otherwise noted, is derived from the report of Sergeant John Mott to Captain Moore dated May 20, 1871.) The purpose of this scout was to determine "the general direction and trails made by large bodies of Indians."[2] One can only imagine Cushing's elation at leading at least a small portion of his former command. Second in command of the detachment was Sergeant John Mott. Others in the party included Acting Corporal John Kilmartin and Privates William Bahans, William Bender, William Chapman, Samuel Cupp, Herman Fichter, Martin Green, Thomas Harrington, John Leffler, Thomas Martin, Daniel Miller, Michael Oherne, Gilman Philbrick, George Pierce, William Soloman and John Yount.[3]

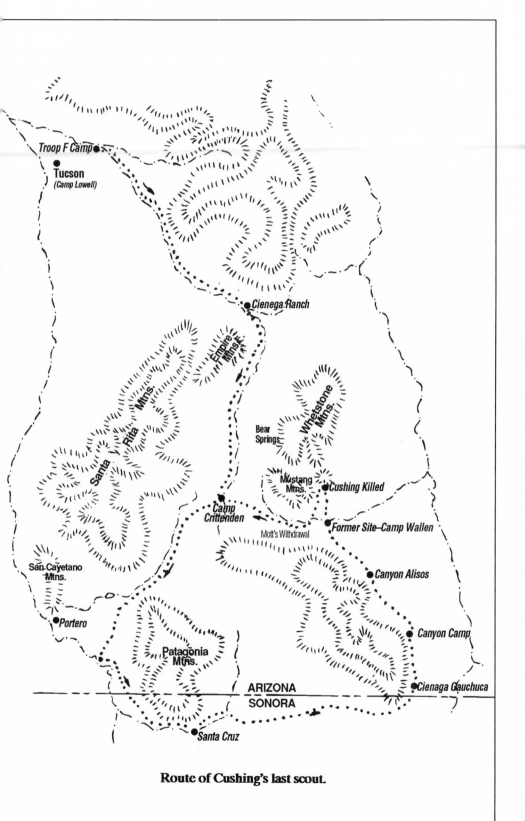

Route of Cushing's last scout.

Also accompanying the detachment was, as allowed by the original orders, a citizen packer, William H. Simpson. Simpson, Cushing's friend, was assigned to be in charge of the small pack train carrying supplies. Simpson's past, as derived from the recollections of local citizens, was somewhat checkered. He claimed to be born in England and educated in France. As a young man, he migrated to the Pacific Northwest and became engaged in the fur trade. His health forced him to move to South America, notably Chile and Peru. From those countries he moved north to Sonora, Mexico. In Sonora, he allegedly owned and worked silver mines until the difficulty of operating a business in Mexico forced him north to the United States. Since his return to this country he had been prospecting the mountains around Tucson.[4]

Departing from their camp on the Rillito on April 27, and marching southeast, their first night's camp was at the Cienega Ranch. The following day they moved to Camp Crittenden located between the present towns of Sonoita and Patagonia. Having marched sixty-five miles in the previous two days, they remained at Crittenden on April 29 to rest their mounts. On April 30, they left Crittenden and proceeded to Portero, Arizona Territory. Upon leaving Portero on May 1, they were guided by Pete Kitchen, owner of a ranch near Portero, who volunteered to lead them through the Santa Rita Mountains to the Santa Cruz River Valley. About 3:00 p.m., Mr. Kitchen left the party to return to his ranch. Shortly thereafter Cushing and Mott, looking behind them, observed that grass had been set on fire, a common Apache tactic to warn other Indians of the approach of Federal troops. It was determined later that Mr. Kitchen had set fire to the grass as a warning they were being followed by a party of Indians. That evening they arrived at Santa Cruz, Mexico, and camped near the Mexican garrison there. It was here that Cushing learned from the Mexican Commandante that there were Indians in the Huachuca Mountains.

On May 2 the troop left Santa Cruz and marched northeast to the Huachuca Mountains, setting up camp at 3:00 p.m. The next day they marched due north along the east slope of the mountains, and near their camp that evening fresh moccasin tracks were found, making it apparent their presence was known. On May 4 they marched over broken and rocky country and set up camp in Cañon Alisos. Since much of the grass had been burned off, this was not a desirable place to stay because there was very little in the way of forage for the animals. Cushing determined to move the next day to the site of an abandoned army post, Camp Wallen, along the banks of the Rio Babocomari.

Upon reaching the site of this deserted camp, they discovered that the grass had not only been burned, but much of it was still burning. Cushing was faced with three choices. He could either return as he had come, go west to Camp Crittenden, or press on to the next available water source, Bear Springs, in the Whetstone Mountains ahead. The burning grass was ample evidence of Indians in the near vicinity but Cushing made the decision to proceed north to Bear Springs. Unbeknownst to the small party, a trap had been set and they were riding into ambush.

About two miles north of Old Camp Wallen, the troop struck a trail of an Indian woman leading a pony and headed in the general direction of their destination. Cushing ordered Sergeant Mott to take three men, Privates Chapman, Green and Pierce, and follow the track while he moved on with the remainder of the party. Mott and his men followed the track for about three-fourths of a mile and entered a deep arroyo or dry water course. Following the trail it became obvious to Mott that the woman was leaving a distinct track, avoiding stones and rocky places to leave a trail in the soft sand. A study of the Department of the Interior Geological Survey Map, Fort Huachuca Quadrangle, sets the scene for what was to follow.[5] Today, the arroyo drops one-hundred fifty-two feet from its inception to its end in a gravel pit. About one-half mile to the north lies the southern end of the Whetstone Mountains and about one-half mile to the southwest is the eastern end of a series of large rock outcroppings called the Mustang Mountains.

While Mott was following the obvious trail, Cushing pushed on with the pack train and the remainder of his men through the gap afforded by the two mountain ranges. After trailing for

a short time, Mott concluded they were being led into a trap
and abandoned the track to warn Cushing. As the four men
climbed the steep wall of this deep gash in the earth, about
fifteen Indians were sighted in a small side slash of the arroyo
waiting to come upon Mott's rear had he continued on the
track. Mott concluded that he and two other men could hold off
this small group, so he dispatched Private Chapman to notify
Cushing of his action. Dismounting to meet this present threat,
they observed a much larger party of Indians running to their
rear. Deeming it necessary to retreat in the face of this much
greater threat, Mott, Green and Pierce attempted to remount.
A volley of fire from the Indians wounded Green's horse and
another shot wounded Pierce. Green and Pierce started on foot
to the rear, the hostiles coming close enough to Green to snatch
the hat from his head. Private Chapman, who had been sent
back to warn Cushing, paused long enough to fire into the war
party. The Indians, perhaps thinking that reinforcements had
arrived, paused in their attack. Realizing that this was not the
case, they resumed their attack, advancing in two lines. The
Apaches in the front line did not stop to reload but advanced
steadily while the second line kept up a harassing fire. Mott's
report indicates that had the attackers so desired, the entire
detachment would have been wiped out.

Cushing soon arrived with the rest of the detachment to aid
the three men. Their appearance drove the Indians back into
the hills, allowing Private Green to escape from the Indians
surrounding him and rejoin his comrades. At this point, the
entire detachment mounted an attack on the hostiles, killing
five of the attackers. Cushing then ordered five Privates, Mott,
and Mr. Simpson to stay with him and ordered the remainder
back to protect the pack train. Thus, with a total of eight men,
he proposed to hold off the war party. Mott, realizing the difficulty of advancing over open ground against a foe he estimated
outnumbered the soldiers fifteen to one, questioned the advis-
ability of moving toward the Apaches securely entrenched
behind natural protective cover. Simpson also cautioned against
any advance. Cushing must have thought his small force had
routed the larger number of Indians. Counting the number with
him said, "Eight, that ought to be enough." This statement is

astonishing, given the position and number of the adversaries. Was Cushing blinded by his past successes? Did he really think that seven men with single shot carbines, probably the Improved Sharps, and percussion-type revolvers along with Mr. Simpson's Henry could defeat a war party of over one hundred hostile Indians? No one has ever questioned Cushing's bravery in his past achievements. However, there is sometimes that fine line between bravery and recklessness. Perhaps Cushing's reckless nature took hold and he ordered his men to advance on the entrenched Indians.

As the men moved forward for about twenty yards, the Apaches laid down a devastating hail of fire. A bullet from the first volley struck Simpson in the head. Cushing ordered Private Yount to Simpson's aid, reducing the small force to six. The Indians, seeing the number was now reduced, rushed from cover at the remaining small group. Cushing was about fifteen feet to Mott's rear when the sergeant heard him cry out, "Sergeant, I am killed! Take me out! Take me out!" Mott turned to see his lieutenant clasp his hand to his chest and fall face forward toward the rear. Calling to Private Fichter to assist him, Mott seized Cushing under one arm and Fichter the other and they began to drag their fallen leader toward the horses. After they had gone only a few steps, Cushing was mortally shot through the head. The two men continued to drag the lifeless officer's body until they came abreast of Private Yount and Mr. Simpson. At this point another Apache bullet entered Simpson's body, killing him. Dropping Cushing's body, Mott and Fichter turned to fire into the advancing hostiles. This brief respite in the Indian charge enabled Privates Green and Yount to mount their horses. Acting Corporal Kilmartin and a portion of the pack train guard now returned to the scene of the battle and opened fire. Mott and Fichter attempted to mount but both horses were wounded, Fichter's in the flank and Mott's in the foreleg. The same volley killed Private Green. Mott's horse could not be ridden, so mounting Cushing's horse, Mott began to direct a retreat.

The nearest place of safety was Camp Crittenden, some seventeen and one-half miles in a direct line from their point of contact with the Indians. However, the Mustang Mountains intervened, making the path to sanctuary much longer. Attempting to keep the pack train with them, as attested by the fact that four mules were lost that could not keep up the pace, a running battle ensued for about a mile. The Indians were drawn from cover and the detachment halted briefly to stand and fight. The Apaches did not accept this latest challenge from the troops. Had they chosen to take up the gauntlet, their superior numbers surely would have prevailed. Mott, a veteran of the Indian Wars, assumed correctly that the Indian leader would prefer to ambush him and his men on the way to Crittenden. Quickly leading his men westward, they crossed the Rio Babocomari about four miles west of Old Camp Wallen in a marshy area near the headwaters of the stream. After safely crossing, they observed the Indians on the eastern side of the watery waste yelling defiantly. With darkness soon approaching, the Apaches broke off the chase. Mott perhaps felt more secure in his escape in the knowledge that Apaches seldom fought at night. He successfully led his party over the rolling hills to Camp Crittenden, arriving there at about 1:00 a.m. on May 6, 1871. The loss to the troop was Lieutenant Howard Cushing, Private Martin Green, and civilian William Simpson. Wounded in the encounter was Private George Pierce.

At that time, the attack on Cushing and his men was widely attributed to the Apache leader, Cochise. However the war party was most certainly led by Juh (Who or Wha). Juh's son, Asa Daklugie, always insisted that "His father led the force that killed Cushing."[6] Daklugie also avowed that his father had a long-standing hatred for Cushing following the incident in the Guadalupe Mountains of New Mexico when Troop F had attacked a Mescalero Indian camp. Although not of his tribe, Juh decried this senseless killing of women and children. Biding his time, Juh waited to lure Cushing into ambush.[7] Although never confirmed, another to-be-famous Apache, Geronimo, was probably a member of the war party. Juh, who suffered from a serious stuttering problem, often had Geronimo speak for him at council fires. Further proof of Juh's leadership of the hostiles was Mott's description of the leader of the attackers. He accurately described Juh, and not Cochise.

After the detachment's arrival at Crittenden, a courier was immediately dispatched to Moore's camp outside Tucson. Moore, along with Second Lieutenant John Bourke and thirty-nine enlisted men left immediately for the scene.[8] As they passed through Tucson, Moore made arrangements for a camp guard consisting of men from Company D, Twenty-first Infantry, stationed at Camp Lowell.[9] Arriving at the scene that afternoon, Troop F found the bodies of Cushing, Green, and Simpson where they had fallen, stripped of their clothing.[10] Sadly they buried the bodies of their fallen comrades where they lay.

At the same time as Cushing's scout, Captain Frank Stanwood, with forty enlisted men of Troop H, Third Cavalry, had been scouting in the same general area although neither knew of the other's presence.[11] This happenstance was not unusual since Troop F operated independently and was not required to coordinate with other troops not under the same orders. We can only speculate on the Indian war party's choice to attack Cushing's small detachment as opposed to Stanwood's larger numbers. The Apaches were certainly aware of both groups. Was the attack on Cushing's group just a sure victory over a small number of men or was Daklugie's boast that his father vowed to kill Cushing the true motive for luring this small detachment into ambush?

After seeing to the burial of their friends, Troop F, in conjunction with Stanwod and his men, began an intense search for the Apache raiders but to no avail. The Indians had used their age-old method of splitting into small groups and heading south across the Arizona-Sonora line only to meet again at a predetermined place in Mexico. Treaty obligations of the time denied United States troops the privilege of pursuit across the international boundary. A search of the area north of the ambush site by a detail from Camp Bowie also proved to be unsuccessful. Thus, any act of retaliation against the Apache war party was thwarted. Troop F returned to their camp on the Rillito on May 12, 1871, minus many of Cushing's men who remained at Camp Crittenden to rest both themselves and their exhausted horses.[12]

The immediate response from the troops stationed at Camp Crittenden may be held in question. However, Crittenden was manned by thirty-six men of the Twenty-first Infantry, Company K, and led by an inexperienced officer, Second Lieutenant William Ross. Infantry would have been useless against mounted Indians. Ross was so inexperienced that Cushing's death and the visit of Moore and Stanwood's commands were not even noted in the Record of Events, as required on the monthly Post Returns.[13]

Except for his family and friends, Cushing's death was hardly noticed by the nation. The passing of one army officer in the Southwest was just one more insignificant event in the course of the nation's history. Although five of his men received Medals of Honor for their part in the fight, the contributions of Howard Cushing to the unenviable task of ensuring the safety of the settlers of the West have largely gone unnoticed. Let us not forget what he and other unsung heroes like him did in their brief time on the stage of history.

EPILOGUE

THOSE HE LEFT BEHIND

Each person's death leaves behind those who loved him or otherwise mourned his passing. So it was with Howard Cushing. Cushing's remains were interred four times, the first being a hastily dug grave in the soil of the Rain Valley between the Whetstone and Mustang Mountains. Later in 1871, his body was removed to a cemetery in Tucson and reinterred with full military honors. When the army post was moved seven miles northeast of the town in 1873, the graves were eventually moved to a new cemetery located there. 1891 found Fort (formerly Camp) Lowell being abandoned and the remains in the military cemetery being moved to the Presidio, San Francisco. Here Cushing's body found its last resting place.

Howard's mother, Mary, died in March of 1891, at the age of eighty-four, at the home of her daughter in St. Joseph's, Missouri. She was preceded in death by all her sons: Walter, had died in infancy; Alonzo, on July 3, 1863; Howard, on May 5, 1871; William, on December 17, 1874; and Milton on January 1,

1887. By the time of Milton's death Mary was an invalid in her daughter's home and unable to attend her son's funeral. After the deaths of Alonzo, Howard, and William a sympathetic Congress awarded her a stipend of fifty dollars per month for her sacrifice to the country. Shortly after Howard's death, she received a money order from Lieutenant John Bourke in the amount of one-hundred twelve dollars, the proceeds from the sale of Howard's personal and military effects. It is interesting to note the newspaper accounts concerning the demise of William and Milton. Milton was said to have suffered "an impairment of the mind, a lingering disease caused by the hardships of the service." William suffered from acute sciatic rheumatism and died from "morphine going to the brain."

Perhaps the person who admired Cushing the most was John Bourke, Cushing's second in command for many months. Bourke often mentions his association with and admiration for Cushing in his book *On The Border With Crook*. Bourke left Troop F in the summer of 1871 when he was appointed Aide-de-Camp to General George Crook, Commander of the Department of Arizona. Bourke became disillusioned with the army. Never rising above the rank of captain, he attributed his lack of promotion to the feud that developed between General Crook and General Nelson Miles. Crook served twice in Arizona and in his second term brought an agreement to surrender from the final renegade Apache, Geronimo. However, those in power in Washington did not agree to Crook's terms of amnesty for the Indians. Crook asked to be relieved and was replaced by Miles who effected Geronimo's final capitulation. Thus, the long-distance bickering between the two generals began, and Bourke believed he was a handy scapegoat. Bourke declined two brevets offered him because none had been offered in the names of those he considered to be the true heroes of the Indian Wars. Bourke died on June 6, 1896.

Captain Evan Thomas, with whom Cushing had become embroiled in the incident that led to the court-martial of both, remained in the army. He was killed during the Modoc Wars in 1873.

* * *

Cushing's last commanding officer, Captain Alexander Moore, left the army on August 10, 1879. He had survived a court-martial charging him with disobeying orders and withdrawing his command in the face of an Indian counterattack on the Powder River in Wyoming. He was found innocent of these charges but found guilty to the prejudice of good order and military discipline. His sentence was approved but remitted by President Grant in view of his record in the Civil War. After his resignation, Moore ranched near San Antonio, Texas, with his father-in-law, retired General Daniel Tyler. Moore became wealthy from his improvement of cattle breeds. He died on September 30, 1910.

Sergeant John Mott was discharged from the army and resumed again his given full name of John Mott McMahon. It is not known why Mott did not use his full name in the military, but there are other instances of men in the frontier army dropping their last names while in the service. Mott became an employee of the Army Quartermaster Department in Chicago and later took the field in this capacity with various army expeditions. He was with General Crook during his fight with Indians on the Rosebud. Mott was one of the five men who received the Medal of Honor for their part in Cushing's last fight, the others being Acting Corporal John Kilmartin and Privates Herman Fichter, Daniel Miller and John Yount. Mott died on August 30, 1917.

Fate was not kind to John Kilmartin. Leaving the army in 1873 he moved to Fort Sill, Oklahoma and became a civilian scout for the army. He invested in a partnership in the Whaley Ranch near the Red River in Texas. In May of 1876, while trailing stock thieves, he and his party stopped at the Whaley Ranch overnight, where Kilmartin visited his wife who was employed as a cook. At sometime early the next morning he was murdered in his sleep by Mrs. Kilmartin, who killed him with a pistol shot to the head, presumably in order for her to continue an affair with his partner, Whaley.

*   *   *

Juh, the Apache credited with leading the war party that ambushed Cushing's men, died in 1883 near Casas Grandes, Chihuahua, Mexico. He perished after a fall off a mountain trail credited to, depending on which source can be believed, a heart attack or drunkenness. Geronimo, whose name in the eyes of most Americans is synonymous with the Apaches, surrendered to the army in 1886. His numbers depleted and many of his tribe already on reservations, he gave up the fight and surrendered to General Miles. He and his followers were shipped off to prison in Florida and eventually were allowed to settle at Fort Sill, Oklahoma. Geronimo died at Fort Sill on February 11, 1909.

Thus, we have come full circle from Cushing's birth to death and the passing of those who affected his life the most. Howard Cushing was one of those unsung heroes in American history whose service to his country has gone largely unnoticed and unappreciated.

ENDNOTES

CHAPTER I

1. Theron W. Haight, *Three Wisconsin Cushings*. (Milwaukee: Wisconsin History Commission, 1910), pp. 3-4.
2. Ibid., p. 2.
3. Ibid., p. 4.
4. Ibid.
5. Ibid., p. 6.
6. Ralph Roskie and Charles Van Doren, *Lincoln's Commando*. (New York: Harper and Brothers, 1957), p. 34.
7. Ibid.
8. Ibid.
9. Ibid.
10. Ibid.
11. Ibid., p. 35. Haight, *Three Wisconsin Cushings*, p. 8.
12. Haight, *Three Wisconsin Cushings*, p. 8.
13. Roskie and Van Doren, *Lincoln's Commando*, p. 35.
14. Ibid.
15. Ibid.
16. Haight, *Three Wisconsin Cushings*, p. 9.
17. Ibid.
18. Ibid.
19. Ibid., p. 38.
20. Historical Museum of the Darwin R. Barker Library, Fredonia, N.Y.; New York State Census, 1855.
21. Roskie and Van Doren, *Lincoln's Commando*, p. 40.
22. Haight, *Three Wisconsin Cushings*, p. 21.
23. Roskie and Van Doren, *Lincoln's Commando*, p. 42.
24. Darwin R. Barker Library, Town of Pomfret Assessment Rolls, 1849.
25. Ibid.; Federal Census, 1850.
26. Ibid.; New York State Census, 1855.
27. Ibid.; Fredonia Academy Records, 1852-1853.
28. Fitchburg Historical Society, Fitchburg, Mass., Letter to author from Eleanora F. West, Executive Director.
29. Roskie and Van Doren, *Lincoln's Commando*, p. 43.
30. *Boston City Directory for the Year Ending June 30, 1859.* (Boston: Adams, Sampson and Co., July 1, 1859), p. 108.
31. Haight, *Three Wisconsin Cushings*, p. 25.
32. Ibid., p. 29.
33. *Report of the Adjutant General of the State of Illinois, Volume VIII, Containing Reports for the Years 1861-1866*, Revised by Brigadier General J.N. Reece, Adjutant General. (Springfield: Journal Co., 1901), p. 607.

CHAPTER II

1. National Archives: File for First Lieutenant Howard Cushing, (9W3/18/2/C), Box 27; Cushing to Bvt. Col. C.W. Morgan, Captain, Fourth Artillery, May 16, 1866.
2. National Archives: Regimental Returns, First Illinois Light Artillery, Co. B, November, 1861-December, 1863, (8W3/14/35/B), Box 109, April 1, 1862.
3. General Henry Hunt, *Journal of the Military Service Institution of the United States*, "Our Experience in Artillery Administration", Vol. XII, March, 1891.
4. Fairfax Downey, *South of the Guns*. (New York: David McKay Co. Inc., 1955), p. 121.
5. Mark Boatner III, *The Civil War Dictionary*. (New York: David McKay Company, Inc., 1988), p. 578; Joseph Roberts, *The Handbook of Artillery, 10th Edition*. (New York: D. Van Nostrand Co., Inc., 1975), p. 114.

6. National Archives: Regimental Returns...September 1, 1862.

7. David G. Martin, *The Shiloh Campaign, March-April, 1862*. (New York: Fairfax Press, 1987), p. 79.

8. Boatner, *The Civil War Dictionary*..., p. 119.

9. National Archives: File for Cushing. Cushing to Morgan, May 16, 1866.

10. *Report of the Adjutant General of the State of Illinois, Volume VIII, Containing Reports for the Years 1861-1866*, Revised by Brigadier General J.N. Reece, Adjutant General. (Springfield: Journal Co., 1901), p. 607.

11. *Report of the Adjutant General of the State of Illinois*..., p. 662.

12. David G. Martin, *The Shiloh Campaign*..., pp. 168-169.

13. *The War of the Rebellion, A Compilation of the Official Records of the Union and Confederate Armies*, Volume XXIV, Series L. (Washington: Government Printing Office, 1897), p. 24.

14. National Archives: Regimental Returns...May 1, 1862.

15. David Martin, *The Shiloh Campaign*..., p. 79.

16. *Boston Post Express*, June 18, 1898.

17. National Archives: Regimental Returns...May 1, 1862.

18. David Martin, *The Shiloh Campaign*..., p. 79.

19. *Boston Post Express*, June 18, 1898.

20. Ibid.; National Archives: Regimental Returns...May 1, 1862.

21. National Archives: Regimental Returns...May 1, 1862.

22. *Boston Post Express*, June 18, 1898.

23. National Archives: Regimental Returns...May 1, 1862.

24. Ibid., August 1, 1862.

25. Ibid., February 1, 1863.

26. National Archives: File for Cushing, Cushing to Morgan.

27. National Archives: Regimental Returns...February 1, 1863.

28. Ibid., April 30, 1863.

29. *The War of the Rebellion*, p. 245.

30. Ibid., p. 246.

31 John F. Marszalek, *Sherman, A Soldier's Passion for Order*. (New York: The Free Press, a Division of MacMillen, Inc., 1993), p. 22.

32. *The War of the Rebellion*, pp. 261-262.

33. Richard Wheeler, *The Siege of Vicksburg*. (New York: Thomas Crowell Co., 1978), p. 149

34. *The War of the Rebellion*, pp. 261-262.

35. National Archives: Regimental Returns...June 1, 1863.

36. Ibid.

37. Ibid., June 30, 1863.

38. Ibid., July 31, 1863.

39. National Archives: File for Cushing, Cushing to Secretary of War Stanton.

40. Ibid., Rumsey's endorsement.

41. Ibid., Taylor's endorsement.

42. Ibid., Lincoln's endorsement.

43. Ibid., Milton Cushing to Stanton.

44. Ibid.

45. Ibid., Assistant Secretary of the Navy Fox to Stanton.

46. National Archives: Regimental Returns...September 30, 1863.

47. Ibid., October 31, 1863.

48. Ibid., November 30, 1863.

49. Ibid.

CHAPTER III

1. National Archives: File for First Lieutenant Howard Cushing (9W3/18/2/C) Box 37, Cushing to Thomas, December 8, 1863.

2. National Archives: Reports of the Fourth United States Artillery, December, 1863-September, 1867, Micro Copy Number 722, Roll Number 29, January, 1864.

3. Ibid.

4. Ibid.

5. Gregory James and the Editors of Time-Life Books, *The Killing Ground, Wilderness to Cold Harbor*. (Alexandria, Va.: Time-Life Books, 1986), p. 114.

6. Ibid.

7. Ibid.

8. Ibid., p. 115.

9. National Archives: Reports of the Fourth United States Artillery...May, 1864.

10. Gregory James, et al: *The Killing Ground...*, p. 115.

11. Ibid.

12. Ibid., p. 122.

13. National Archives: Reports of the Fourth United States Artillery...May, 1864.

14. Ibid.

15. Ray Morris, Jr., *Sheridan, The Life and Wars of General Phillip Sheridan*. (New York: Crown Publishing, 1992), p. 169.

16. Ibid.

17. Gregory James, et al, *The Killing Ground...*, p. 118.

18. National Archives: Reports of the Fourth United States Artillery...May, 1864.

19. Ibid.

20. National Archives: File for First Lieutenant Howard Cushing, Cushing to Morgan, May 16, 1866.

21. National Archives: Reports of the Fourth United States Artillery...June, 1864.

22. Theron W. Haight, *Three Wisconsin Cushings*, p. 91.

23. National Archives: Special Order No. 112, September 4, 1864, Headquarters, Inspector of Artillery, United States Army.

24. Frank Wilkenson, *Recollections of a Private Soldier in the Army of the Potomac*. (New York, 1887), pp. 223-224, as reprinted in Haight, *Three Wisconsin Cushings*.

25. National Archives: Reports of the Fourth United States Artil-lery...September, 1865.

CHAPTER IV

1. National Archives: Reports of the Fourth United States Artillery, December, 1863-September, 1867, Micro Copy Number 722, Roll Number 29, September, 1865.

2. National Archives: Case MM3265 (Thomas, King) Box 1350. Testimony of Walter Thompson.

3. Ibid.

4. Ibid., Testimony of Private George Samisel.

5. Ibid., Testimony of AAS Henry Armstrong.

6. Ibid., Testimony of Second Lieutenant Howard Cushing.

7. National Archives: Findings of the Court of Inquiry (Thomas, King) Case 3265, Box 1350.

8. National Archives: Case MM3549 (H.B. Cushing) Box 1416, Testimony of David Cunningham.

9. Ibid.

10. Ibid., Testimony of Officer Jeffery Robinson.

11. Ibid.

12. *Revised United States Army Regulations of 1861, With an Appendix Containing the Laws Affecting Army Regulations and Articles of War to June 25, 1863*. (Washington: Government Printing House, 1863), Article 92.

13. National Archives: Case MM3265 (Thomas, King) Box 1350, Testimony of First Lieutenant Rufus King.

14. National Archives: Case MM3549 (H.B. Cushing) Box 1416.

15. Chautauqua County Historical Society, Westfield, N.Y.: Cushing Family Collection, Undated Letter, Milton to Mary Cushing.

16. National Archives: Case MM3549 (H.B. Cushing) Box 1416, Sentence of the Court.

17. National Archives: Special Order No. 103, Adjutant General's Office, War Department, April 17, 1866.

18. National Archives: Case MM3549 (H.B. Cushing) Box 1416, Cushing to President Johnson.

19. National Archives: Reports of the Fourth United States Artil-lery...January, 1867.

20. National Archives: Case MM3549 (H.B. Cushing) Box 1416, Townsend to Cushing, May 26, 1867.

CHAPTER V

1. *Revised United States Army Regulations of 1861...* Article IV, par. 30-32.

2. National Archives: File for First Lieutenant Howard Cushing, (9W3/18/2/C), Box 37, Cushing to Adjutant General.

3. Ibid., Thomas endorsement.

4. Ibid., Canby endorsement.

5. Ibid., Cushing request.

6. Ibid., Canby endorsement.

7. Ibid., Cushing request for withdrawal of transfer.

8. Ibid., Ruger, denial of transfer.

9. Ibid., Roberts, denial of transfer.

10. Ibid., Requests of Cushing and Dixon.

11. National Archives: Special Order No. 437, Headquarters of the Army, Adjutant General's Office, September 7, 1867.

12. *Army-Navy Journal*, April 25, 1868, p. 570.

13. National Archives: File for First Lieutenant Howard Cushing...Oath of Office.

14. National Archives: Returns from United States Army Regiments, Third Cavalry 1863-1875, July 30, 1868 to January 6, 1869.

15. *Handbook of American Indians*, edited by Frederick Hodge. (Totona, N.Y.: Rowan and Littlefield, 1975), p. 63.

16. National Archives: Bimonthly Muster Reports, Third Cavalry, Troop F, August 31-October 31, 1868.

CHAPTER VI

1. John G. Bourke: *On the Border With Crook.* (New York: Charles Scribner's Sons, 1891. Reprinted by University of Nebraska Press, Lincoln, 1971), p. 30.

2. National Archives: Bimonthly Muster Report, Third Cavalry, Troop F, August 31-October 31, 1868; National Archives: Returns from United States Army Regiments, Third Cavalry, February 26, 1869.

3. Adjutant General's Office: *Chronological List of Actions, etc. With Indians from January, 1837 to January, 1891*, Introduction by Dale E. Floyd. (Fort Collins, Colorado: Old Army Press, 1979), p. 38.

4. National Archives: Bimonthly Muster Report, Troop F, October 31-December 31, 1868.

5. Ibid.; National Archives: Returns from United States Army Regiments, Third Cavalry, February 26, March 19, and March 26, 1869.

6. National Archives: Returns from United States Army regiments, Third Cavalry, March 26, 1869.

7. Ibid.

8. Adjutant General's Office: *Chronological List of Actions, etc.*, p. 38.

9. National Archives: Bimonthly Muster Report, Troop F, December 31, 1868 to February 28, 1869.

10. National Archives: Bimonthly Muster Report, Troop F, February 28 to April 30, 1869.

11. Adjutant General's Office: *Chronological List of Actions, etc.*, p. 39.

12. National Archives: Bimonthly Muster Report, Troop F, April 30 to June 30 1869.

13. National Archives: Bimonthly Muster Report, Troop F, June 30 to August 31, 1869; National Archives: Returns of United States Army Regiments, Third Cavalry, September 30, 1869; Adjutant General's Office: *Chronological List of Actions, etc.*, p. 42.

14. National Archives: Bimonthly Muser Report, Troop F, August 31 to October 30, 1869.

15. Ibid., October 30 to December 31, 1869; Adjutant General's Office: *Chronological List of Actions, etc.*, p. 43.

16. National Archives: Bimonthly Muster Report, Troop F, October 30 to December 31, 1869.

17. John Bourke: *On the Border with Crook*, p. 29; National Archives: Bimonthly Muster Report, Troop F, October 30 to December 31, 1869; Adjutant General's Office: *Chronological List of Actions, etc.*, p. 44.

18. Dan Thrapp: *Juh, An Incredible Indian.* (El Paso: Texas Western Press, The University of Texas at El Paso, 1973), Eve Ball to Thrapp, October 5, 1957, p. 10.

19. National Archives: Returns of United States Army Regiments, Third Cavalry, February 1870.

20. John Bourke: *On the Border with Crook*, p. 3.

21. National Archives: Bimonthly Muster Report, Troop F, December 31, 1869 to February 28, 1870; Dale F. Giese, *Echoes of the Bugle* (Silver City, N.M.: Phelps Dodge Corp. 1991), p. 24.

22. National Archives: Bimonthly Muster Report, Troop F, February 28 to April 30, 1870.

23. John Bourke, *On the Border with Crook*, p. 4.

24. National Archives: Bimonthly Muster Report, Troop F, April 30 to June 30, 1871.

25. Ibid.

26. John Bourke, *On the Border with Crook*, p. 27.

27. National Archives: Bimonthly Muster Report, Troop F, April 30 to June 30, 1870; Adjutant General's Office: *Chronological List of Actions, etc.*, p. 45.

28. John Bourke, *On the Border with Crook*, p. 32.

29. Ibid., p. 38.

30. Adjutant General's Office: *Chronological List of Actions, etc.*, p. 46.

31. John Bourke, *On the Border with Crook*, p. 42.

32. Ibid., p. 43; National Archives: Bimonthly Muster Report, Troop F, June 30 to August 31, 1870; Adjutant General's Office: *Chronological List of Actions, etc.*, p. 46.

33. National Archives: Department of Arizona, Special Order No. 74, August 9, 1870. E. W. Stone to Cushing.

34. National Archives: Bimonthly Muster Report, Troop F, June 30 to August 31, 1870.

CHAPTER VII

1. John G. Bourke, *On the Border with Crook*, p. 57.

2. Ibid., p. 57.

3. Ibid., pp. 45-46.

4. National Archives: Bimonthly Muster Report, Third Cavalry, Troop F, August 31 to October 31, 1870; National Archives: Returns from United States Army Regiments, Third Cavalry, September, 1870.

5. John G. Bourke, *On the Border with Crook*, p. 98.

6. National Archives: Bimonthly Muster Report, Troop F, August 31 to September 30, 1870; National Archives: Returns from United States Army Regiments, Third Cavalry, September, 1870.

7. National Archives: Bimonthly Muster Report, Troop F, August 31 to September 30, 1870.

8. National Archives: Returns from United States Army Regiments, Third Cavalry, October 1870; Adjutant General's Office, *Chronological List of Actions With*

Indians, etc., from January, 1837 to January, 1891. Introduction by Dale E. Floyd (Fort Collins, CO.: The Old Army Press, 1979), p. 47.

9. National Archives: Bimonthly Muster Report, Troop F, October 31 to December 31, 1870; National Archives: Returns of United States Army Regiments, Third Cavalry, December 1870.

10. Ibid.; Ibid.; *Chronological List of Actions, etc.*, p. 47.

11. National Archives: Bimonthly Muster Report, Troop F, October 31 to December 31, 1870; National Archives: Returns of United States Army Regiments, Third Cavalry, December 1870.

12. Ibid.; Ibid.

13. National Archives: Bimonthly Muster Report, Troop F, December 31, 1870 to February 28, 1871; National Archives: Returns of United States Army Regiments, Third Cavalry, February 1870; *Chronological List of Actions, etc.*, p. 47.

14. Dan Thrapp, *Encyclopedia of Frontier Biography.* (Glendale, CA.: Arthur Clark Co., 1988), p. 1009; National Archives: Register of Enlistments, 1866, Volume 63, Entry 2673, p. 252.

15. National Archives: Bimonthly Muster Report, Troop F, December 31, 1870 to February 28, 1871.

16. National Archives: Returns of United States Army Regiments, Third Cavalry, December, 1870 and January, 1871.

17. National Archives: File for First Lieutenant Howard Cushing (9W3/18/2/C), Box 21, Denial of Brevet, Grant to Schofield.

18. National Archives: Bimonthly Muster Report, Troop F, December 31, 1870 to February 28, 1871.

19. Ibid., February 28 to April 30, 1871; *Chronological List of Actions, etc.*, p. 48.

20. Ibid.; Ibid.

21. Ibid.; Ibid.

22. Dan Thrapp, *Encyclopedia of Frontier Biography*, p. 1009; Dan Thrapp, *The Conquest of Apacheria*. (Norman and London: University of Oklahoma Press, 1967), p. 98.

23. National Archives: DeAnne Blanton to author, January 24, 1994.

24. National Archives: Bimonthly Muster Report, Troop F, February 28 to April 30, 1871.

CHAPTER VIII

1. National Archives: Adjutant General's Office 187, F/W 1959. Adjutant General's Office, 1871 - Report of Sergeant John Mott to Captain Alexander Moore, May 20, 1871.

2. *Arizona Citizen*, May 20, 1871.

3. National Archives: Bimonthly Muster Report, Third Cavalry, Troop F, February 28 to April 30, 1871.

4. *Arizona Citizen*, May 13, 1871.

5. United States Department of the Interior, Geological Survey Map, Fort Huachuca Quadrangle.

6. Dan Thrapp, *Juh, An Incredible Indian*.

7. Eve Ball with Nora Hern and Linda Sanchez, *Indeh, An Apache Odyssey*. (Provo: Brigham Young University Press, 1980), p. 26.

8. National Archives: Bimonthly Muster Report, Troop F, February 28 to April 30, 1871 (Number based on personnel available as of April 30, 1871).

9. National Archives: Post Returns for Fort Lowell, January, 1866 to December 1877. Micro Film Number 617-513. May 30, 1871.

10. John G. Bourke, *On the Border With Crook*, p. 106.

11. National Archives: Post Returns for Camp Grant, October, 1865 to March, 1879. Record Group Number 94. April 30, 1871 and May 31, 1871.

12. National Archives: Post Returns for Camp Crittenden, Micro Copy Number 617, Roll Number 267, May 31, 1871.

13. Ibid.

EXHIBIT A
First Illinois Light Artillery Records

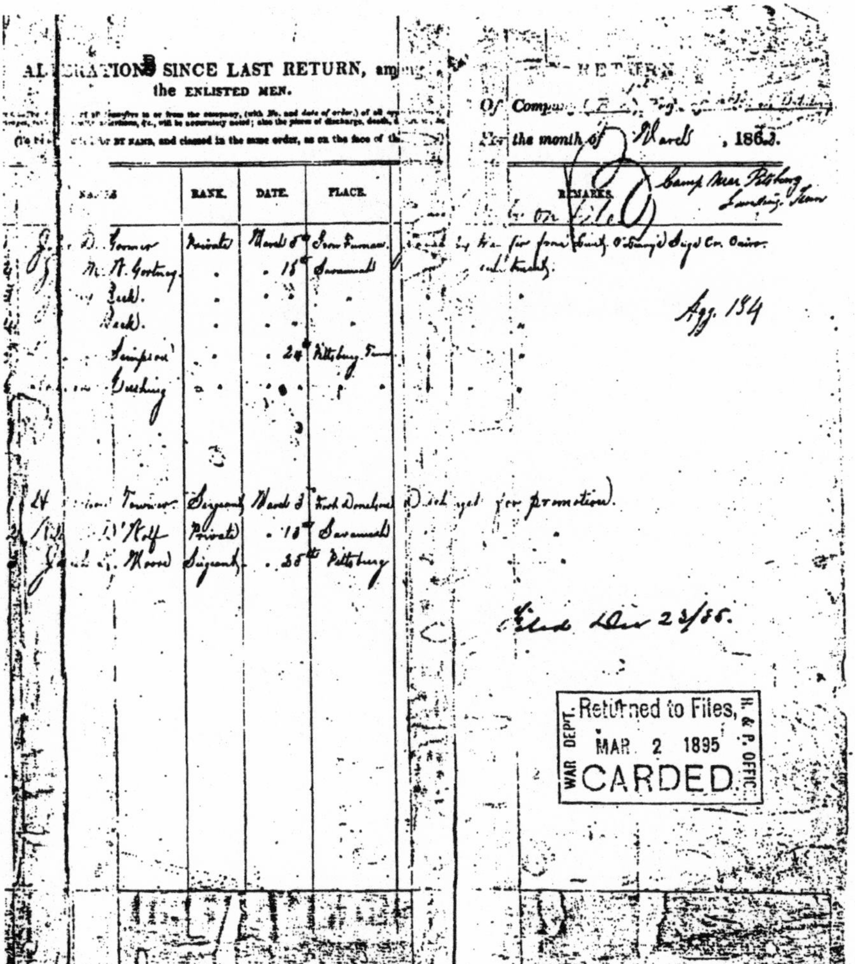

EXHIBIT B
First Illinois Light Artillery Records

| *C* | **1** L. Art'y. | **Ill.** |

Howard Cushing

Pvt., Batt'y B, 1 Reg't Illinois L. Art'y.

Appears on

Battery Muster Roll

for *May & June*, 186 *2*

Present or absent *Present*

Stoppage, $ 100 for

Due Gov't, $ 100 for

Valuation of horse, $ 100

Valuation of horse equipments, $ 100

Remarks: *Mussed m pay (Enrolled & m/in at Chicago Mar 24/62 for 3 yrs)*

Book mark:

Bryan

(358) Copyist.

EXHIBIT C
First Illinois Light Artillery Records

FIRST ARTILLERY. 607

Name and Rank.	Residence.	Date of rank or en-listment.	Date of muster.	Remarks.
Burnam, Arthur........	Chicago	July 21,1861	July 21,1861	M. O. July 23, '64, as Corp'l.
Briggs, William D.....	``	Aug. 30,1861	Aug. 30,1861	Re-enlisted as Veteran....
Beidelman, Alex. H...	``	Jan. 20,1862	Jan. 20,1862	Assigned to new Bat. A....
Beck, John..............	Iuka, Miss......	Mar. 18,1862	May 18,1862	`` ``
Beck, Jeffrey	``		``	Disch. Mar. 2, '63; disabil...
Brown, John A........	Chicago	Aug. 5,1862	Aug. 5,1862	Assigned to new Bat. A....
Bradbury, William H..	``	Aug. 6,1862	Aug. 6,1862	
Bower, Michael.......	``	Aug. 7,1862	Aug. 7,1862	`` `` ....
Beckers, Oscar E.......	``	Aug. 29,1861	Aug. 29,1861	Killed at Fort Donelson, Feb. 13, 1862.........
Ball, Zebina M........	``	July 25,1861	July 25,1861	Died, St.Louis, May 14,1862.
Blaikes, William......	``	July 30,1861	July 30,1861	Disch. Oct. 31, '62; disabil..
Brickbill, William.....	``	July 21,1861	July 21,1861	M. O. July 23, '64, as Corp'l.
Blaisdell, Timothy M.	``	July 25,1861	July 25,1861	Prom. 1st Sgt., then 1st Lt.
Burns, George B.......	Rockford	Dec. 23,1863	Dec. 23,1863	Assigned to new Co. A....
Clark, Henry R........	Chicago........	July 26,1861	July 26,1861	Mustered out July 23,1864..
Chatfield, John, Jr....	``	Aug. 22,1861	Aug. 22,1861	Died at Bridgeport, Ala., Nov. 23, 1863..............
Cushing, Howard B...	``	Mar. 24,1862	Mar. 24,1862	Disch. Nov.30,'63, for prom.
Cobb, Henry B	``	Aug. 2,1862	Aug. 2,1862	Assigned to new Co. A....
Chalman, John P.....	``	Aug. 5,1862	Aug. 5,1862	`` `` ....
Crego, William D	``	July 23,1861	July 23,1861	M. O. July 23,'64, as Serg't.
Coe, Schuyler P	``	Sept. 17,1861	Sept. 17,1861	Assigned to new Co. A....
Cutting, John T.......	``	July 24,1861	July 24,1861	Disch. July 7, '62; disabil...
Clark, Charles H.......	Rock Creek.....	Nov. 17,1863	Dec. 31,1864	Assigned to new Co. A....
Crampton, Franklin...	Rockford	Dec. 23,1863	Dec. 23.1863	`` `` ....

EXHIBIT D
Cushing's Letter to Secretary of War Stanton

Sherman's Army Corps
Camp of Co "B" 1st Ills Artillery
August 5th 1862.

Sir:—

I beg respectfully to state that I have been connected with Company "B" Chicago Light Artillery since March 1862, participating in the Battles of Shiloh, Siege of Corinth, battles of Chickasaw Bayou, Arkansas Post, and the Siege and Capture of Vicksburg, and also in several skirmishes, and in many arduous Marches, and have acquired I think, a good Knowledge of the drill and discipline of the Artillery Service.—

My younger brother 1st Lt Alonzo H. Cushing late Commander of Battery "A" 4th Regt U.S. Artillery fell at the Battle of Gettysburg: And I now most respectfully apply for a Commission in the same Regiment and, if possible, an appointment to the same Battery to which my brother was attached, confident that should this honor be conferred upon me, it will prove no loss to the Government.—

I have the honor to be, Sir:
Very Respectfully your Obt Servt
Howard Cushing

EXHIBIT E
Rumsey's Letter to Secretary of War Stanton

Headquarters Co. B. 1st Reg't Illinois L't Artillery,
Camp near Big Black River, Miss. August 5th 1863.

I take pleasure in recommending Private Howard Cushing of my Battery for an appointment to a position in the U.S. Artillery Service, as per his application herewith. He has been in the Service as a soldier in my Battery since March 1862, and has given, in that time, good proofs of his bravery and courage and intelligence at the battles of Shiloh, Chickasaw Bayou and Post of Arkansas, and during the Sieges of Corinth and Vicksburg. In camp and on the march, he has ever been the faithful soldier, obedient to orders, and attentive to his duties.

He has a good knowledge of the drill, and minutiae of the artillery service, and I think his qualities fit him, in a good degree, for an efficient disciplinarian and officer. His Moral Character is unexceptionable.

In appointing Mr. Cushing to a position in the Regular Army, the President will appoint Secure a good officer, and honor the memory of a noble soldier, who lately fell bravely fighting in his Country's service

Israel P. Rumsey 2nd Lieutenant Commanding
Company B. 1st Light Artillery Reg't of Illinois Volunteers.

EXHIBIT F
Ezra Taylor's Recommendation

Head Quarters 15th Army Corps
Office Chief of Artillery
Camp on Black River. Miss
August 6th 1863

I take great pleasure in endorsing
the within application and recom-
-mendation and have no doubt
if a commission is granted. It
will be the highest aim of the
within named soldier to do honor
to the country which bestows upon
him its honors and confidence.

Ezra Taylor
Major Comdg
1st Ills Light Artillery
Chief of Artillery 15th C. O.

EXHIBIT G
President Abraham Lincoln's Endorsement

First Lieut. (Alonzo H.
Cushing) of Battery A.
4th Reg. U. S. Artillery,
was killed at Gettysburg.
His brother, William B,
Howard Cushing, having
had a great deal of
Artillery practice, as shown
within, asks to fill
the vacancy — or the
ultimate vacancy, in
the case — I know
not whether this can
be consistently done,
but this case seems
a meritorious one.

A Lincoln

Aug. 21. 1863

EXHIBIT H
Milton Cushing's Appeal to Secretary of War Stanton

(Copy)

Navy Dep.
Bureau of Yards & Docks.
Aug 26th 1863

Sir:

An application was presented to your Department, a few days ago, from Howard Cushing, a private in Co. B. 1st Illinois Artillery, (Taylor's well known battery,)—for a commission in the regular Army, endorsed by the Commander of his battery, the chief of artillery of his division, and his Excellency, the President. It was only made after the earnest solicitation of his friends, who desired his promotion for the following reasons, to which I respectfully invite your consideration.— His brother, 1st Lieut Alonzo H. Cushing, late Commander of battery A, 4th U.S. Artillery, after devoting over two years of his life, and his whole soul and energies, to the cause of his country, as you may be aware, fell fighting most heroically at Gettysburg. In his death, his mother, who has given three sons to the service, lost one of the chief props and hopes of her declining years. It was but natural at such a time and occasion, for all who knew the worth of Alonzo Cushing, to desire to have him placed in a position similar to that so nobly filled and honored by his younger brother. But his claims are not based on his brother's service alone. With a good academic education, a long and highly creditable experience in the artillery service, and a heart beaming with patriotism and dread of fear, he is presented by those who know him as one whose merits are sufficient to claim the attention of the War Department, as one who has never quailed before a foe, and who has in him all the elements of a good and courageous officer.

EXHIBIT H cont.

His friends, aware of the large number of appointments that have been made from the volunteer service and civil life, and of those still occasionally being made from the latter, did not suffer themselves to doubt that the high appreciative sense of the Department would recognize the justice of this application.

I do not profess, sir, to be indifferent to the interests of one whose abilities, virtues, and endearing qualities, I have so long known. Nor do I deem it improper that his friends should ask his promotion, in view not only of his own deserts, and his widowed and bereaved mother's sacrifices, but, also, as a tribute to the memory of a gallant officer whose life-blood was so freely poured out in repelling the fierce and insolent invaders from the State of Pennsylvania, and who did not live to enjoy the rewards and honors so fully merited by his conduct.

May it not be hoped, without unwarranted presumption, that the Department will feel justified, under such circumstances, in making an exception to a stringent rule, and confer the appointment asked?

I am, Sir, very respectfully,
Your Obt. Servant,
Milton B. Cushing

Hon. Edwin M. Stanton,
Secretary of War.

EXHIBIT I
Milton Cushing's Appeal to Assistant Secretary of Navy Fox

Washington, Sept 7. 1863.

Memorandum.

On the 21st Aug. last an application was rec'd from Howard Cushing, a private in Co. B. 1st Ill. Artillery. (Taylor's Chicago Battery), for a commission in the regular Army. This application was fully endorsed by Lieut Rumsey - Commander of the battery, and Major Taylor, Chief of Artillery for Gen. Sherman. Admiral Smith took the application to the President, who also endorsed it; after which he took it to the Secretary of War, who said a rule had been adopted by that Dep.t against such promotions. That he would only promote from the regular service. The application was put on file.

On the 26th of Aug. a letter was written to the Sec. of War on the subject, a copy of which is enclosed.

It appears that the difficulty mentioned by Mr Stanton could be overcome, by first discharging the applicant from the volunteer service and then promoting him - or appointing him in the regular

EXHIBIT I cont.

army, as appointments of that nature are still being made. Either the same day, or the day before this application was presented. I am informed that a clerk in the army, who formerly belonged to the "Sturgis Rifles" or "McClellan's body guard", and who was mustered out of service when Gen. McClellan was relieved of his command, – was made a Second Lieut, in the regular army.

Respectfully Your Obdr Servant

W. B. Cushing
Let. U.S.N.

To
Hon. G. V. Fox,
Asst Secretary of Navy,
Washington,
D.C. –

EXHIBIT J
Assistant Secretary Fox's Letter to Colonel James Hardie

Navy Department
September 7th 1863

Dear Sir:

I have just received from Lieut. Wm. B. Cushing, U.S.N. the enclosed Memorandum and copy of letter relative to Howard Cushing's application for a Commission in the regular army and take much pleasure in forwarding them to you. I would respectfully ask if the application has been acted upon and if it has not, and is likely to be unfavorable to Mr. Cushing I desire to see the Secretary of War in regard to it. The case seems to be particularly deserving. I can say, without hesitation, that the writer of the enclosed, Lieut. Wm. B. Cushing, is the most meritorious

young officer in the Navy and has
received the highest commendations
of the officers under whom he has
served. His brother Alonzo a gradu-
ate of West Point, died at his post
~~in the fight at Gettysburg; and now~~
~~the remaining~~ brother, Howard, presents
~~an~~ application, endorsed by the President
also his superior officers, for a position
for which he appears to be qualified.

I have such a high appreciation
of the merits of Lieut. W. B. Cushing that
I cannot help taking great interest
in the welfare of his brother and
should be gratified to learn that his
application has received a favorable
consideration.   Yours very truly.

Col. James A Hardie,   J.D. Fox.
A. A. Gent U. S. Army.

EXHIBIT K
Cushing's Letter of Acceptance to Brigadier General Thomas

Washington, December 8th 1863—

Sir:—

I have the honor to acknowledge, and hereby accept, my appointment by the President of the United States, as a Second Lieutenant in the Fourth Regiment of U.S. Artillery, and enclose herewith the Oath of Office, duly executed.

In conformity with the requirements contained in my appointment, I have to state, that I was born in Milwaukie, Wisconsin, am twenty-five (25) years of age, and was a permanent resident of the State of Illinois prior to my entry into the military service of the United States.

I have the honor, Sir, to be,

Very respectfully,
Your Obt. Servt.
Howard B. Cushing.
2d Lieut. 4th U.S. Artillery

Brigadier Genl. L. Thomas,
Adjutant General U.S.A.,
Washington,

EXHIBIT L
Transcript of Court Martial

II...Before a General Court Martial which convened at Washington, D. C., March 1, 1866, pursuant to Special Orders, No. 32, dated February 9, 1866, and No. 47, dated March 6, 1866, Headquarters, Department of Washington, Washington, and of which Brevet Brigadier-General W. H. EMORY, Colonel, 5th U. S. Cavalry, is President, was arraigned and tried—

2d Lieutenant *Howard B. Cushing*, 4th U. S. Artillery.

CHARGE.—" Conduct to the prejudice of good order and military discipline."

Specification 1st—" In this ; that 2d Lieutenant *Howard B. Cushing*, 4th Regiment United States Artillery, did unlawfully interfere with Jefferson Robinson, a member of the Metropolitan Police of the Third Precinct, Georgetown, D. C., said Robinson then being in the discharge of his duty at the Police Station House of the said Third Precinct of Georgetown, and said Cushing did, in a threatening and insulting manner, say to said Robinson, ' You must give him up ; you will have to give him up ; you know we can take him,' or words to that effect, meaning thereby Captain E. Thomas, 4th U. S. Artillery, and Brevet Major, U. S. A., who was then and there in custody of said

Metropolitan Police at said Station House. This at or near Georgetown, D. C., on or about the 8th day of November, 1865."

Specification 2d—" In this ; that he, 2d Lieutenant *Howard B. Cushing*, 4th Regiment United States Artillery, did, without proper authority, order a part, to wit: sixteen men of Company 'A,' 4th Regiment United States Artillery, said Company 'A,' and said sixteen men of said Company 'A,' 4th Regiment United States Artillery, being at the time by the General Commanding intended for duty and on duty at Fort Whipple, Va., to report in the night time, to wit: about 2 o'clock, A. M., with their arms, to 1st Lieutenant Rufus King, of said regiment, and Brevet Major, U. S. Army, at or near Georgetown, D. C., for duty not connected with Fort Whipple, Va., but for the purpose of effecting the release of Captain Evan Thomas, 4th Regiment United States Artillery, and Brevet Major, U. S. Army, then and there a prisoner in the custody of the civil authorities in Georgetown, D. C.; and for the purpose of arresting stragglers in Georgetown, D. C., meaning thereby soldiers belonging to Company 'A,' 4th Regiment United States Artillery, who might be absent from said Fort Whipple, and in Georgetown, D. C., without the proper authority. This at Fort Whipple, Virginia, on or about the 8th day of November, 1865."

EXHIBIT L cont.

Specification 3d—"In this; that he, 2d Lieutenant *Howard B. Cushing*, 4th Regiment United States Artillery, did, without proper authority, assist 1st Lieutenant Rufus King, 4th United States Artillery, and Brevet Major, U. S. Army, in his unlawful attempt to effect the release from the custody of the civil authorities, Captain Evan Thomas, 4th Regiment United States Artillery, and Brevet Major, U. S. Army, then and there being a prisoner in the said custody of the said civil authorities in Georgetown, D. C., by procuring and ordering improperly and without authority, armed soldiers, to wit: sixteen soldiers belonging to Company 'A,' 4th Regiment United States Artillery, on duty at Fort Whipple, Virginia, to report to 1st Lieutenant Rufus King, 4th Regiment U. S. Artillery, and Brevet Major, U. S. Army, at or near Georgetown, D. C., for the purpose of aiding the said Brevet Major King to effect the release, improperly and without authority, of the said Brevet Major Thomas, a prisoner in Georgetown, D. C., and then and there in the custody of the civil authorities. This at Fort Whipple, Virginia, on or about the 8th day of November, 1865."

Specification 4th—"In this; that 2d Lieutenant *Howard B. Cushing*, 4th Regiment United States Artillery, did, without proper authority, order a large number, to wit: sixteen soldiers of the soldiers belonging to Company 'A.' 4th Regiment United States Artillery, stationed at Fort Whipple, Virginia, and on duty at said Fort Whipple, to report, armed and ready for duty, to Brevet Major Rufus King, at or near Georgetown, D. C., for the purpose of overpowering the Police of Georgetown, D. C., and releasing from confinement Captain Evan Thomas, 4th Regiment United States Artillery, and Brevet Major, U. S. Army, who was there and then in the custody of said Police as a prisoner, charged with the violation of the civil law. This on or about the 8th day of November, 1865."

To which charge and specifications the accused, 2d Lieutenant *Howard B. Cushing*, 4th U. S. Artillery, pleaded "Not Guilty."

FINDING.

The Court, having maturely considered the evidence adduced, finds the accused, 2d Lieutenant *Howard B. Cushing*, 4th U. S. Artillery, as follows:—

Of the 1st *Specification*, "Not Guilty."
Of the 2d *Specification*, "Not Guilty."
Of the 3d *Specification*, "Guilty."
Of the 4th *Specification*, "Guilty."
Of the CHARGE, "Guilty."

EXHIBIT L cont.

SENTENCE.

And the Court does therefore sentence him, 2d Lieutenant *Howard B. Cushing*, 4th U. S. Artillery, "*To be suspended from rank and pay for the term of twelve months.*"

III...The proceedings, findings and sentences of the Court in the foregoing cases of Brevet Major *Rufus King*, 1st Lieutenant, 4th U. S. Artillery, Brevet Major *Evan Thomas*, Captain, 4th U. S.

Artillery, and 2d Lieutenant *Howard B. Cushing*, 4th U. S. Artillery, have been approved by the Department Commander, and submitted to the President for his orders.

In the cases of Brevet Major *Rufus King*, 1st Lieutenant, 4th U. S. Artillery, and Brevet Major *Evan Thomas*, Captain, 4th U. S. Artillery, the sentences are commuted "*To suspension from rank and pay for one (1) year.*"

In the case of 2d Lieutenant *Howard B. Cushing*, 4th U. S. Artillery, the sentence is approved.

BY ORDER OF THE PRESIDENT OF THE UNITED STATES:

E. D. TOWNSEND,
Assistant Adjutant General.

OFFICIAL:

Assistant Adjutant General.

EXHIBIT M
Cushing's Appeal to President Andrew Johnson

Washington, March 29th 1867

To His Excellency

Andrew Johnson,

President

I have the honor to make the

following request and statement.

I most respectfully request that the sentence in my case, as promulgated in Special Order 103, War Dept. A.G.O. dated April 17th 1866 be altered so as to read Suspended from duty, and Command, instead of "Suspended from rank and pay", for the following reason, viz:

Capt. E. Thomas, 4th Arty, 1st St. Rufus King Jr. 4th Arty, Bt. Maj. U.S.A. and myself were arrested together, for participation in the same offence, and were tried by the same Court. Capt. Thomas charged with drunkenness while on duty, conduct unbecoming an officer and a gentleman and assault with intent to kill, and was found guilty of the two last charges and was sentenced to dismissal and hard labor for the period of two years. Maj. King was charged with Conduct unbecoming an officer and a gentleman and was sentenced to be dismissed the same while I was charged only with conduct prejudicial to good order and military

following request and statement.

I most respectfully request that the sentence in my case, as promulgated in Special Order 103, War Dept. A.G.O. dated April 17th 1866 be altered so as to read Suspended from duty, and Command, instead of "Suspended from rank and pay", for the following reason, viz:

EXHIBIT M cont

Capt. E. Thomas, 4 Arty 1st St. Rufus King Jr. 4 Arty. Bvt. Maj. U.S.A. and myself were arrested together for participation in the same affair, and were tried by the same Court. Capt. Thomas charged with drunkenness while on duty, Conduct unbecoming an officer and a gentleman and assault with intent to kill, and was found guilty of the two last charges and was sentenced to dismissal and hard labor for the period of two years. Maj. King was charged with Conduct unbecoming an officer and a gentleman and was sentenced to be dismissed the service while I was charged only with conduct prejudicial to good order and military discipline, and was sentenced to be suspended from rank and pay for the period of Twelve months.

Before the promulgation of the sentences and their bases, those of Capt. Thomas and Maj. King were altered so as to read the same as in mind, although they were found guilty on charges much heavier than were even alleged against me.

From my position in my regiment I have lost much rank while the two officers who were suspended at the same time with me, gained rank during their suspension.

I am, therefore, actually suffering greater punishment than either of them, although as it would seem from the charges, findings and sentences on record in these cases, I was deemed as the least guilty among those implicated.

As the term for which by the sentence before mentioned I was to be suspended it to expire on the 17 of April next I would most respectfully ask action may be taken in my case as soon as may be convenient.

I am, Sir,

Very respectfully,

Your obt. Servt.

Howard B. Cushing

St. A. U.S. Arty

EXHIBIT N
Request by Cushing and Lieutenant Ray for Exchange of Positions

Washington, D.C.

May 6th 1865.

Adjutant General,
United States Army,
Washington, D.C.

General:—

We, the undersigned, mutually request that we may be transferred as follows:—

2d Lieut. Howard B. Cushing from the 4th U.S. Artillery, to the 33d U.S. Infantry.

2d Lieut. P. H. Ray from the 33d U.S. Infantry to the 4th U.S. Artillery.

We are, General,

Very respectfully
Your obt servts,

Howard B. Cushing
2d Lieut 4th U.S. Arty

P H Ray
2d Lieut 33d U.S. Infantry

EXHIBIT O
Brigadier General Roberts Denies Transfer

Hd. Qrs. 3rd U.S. Cavalry
Fort Union N. M.
Sept 25, 1867.

Respectfully returned disapproved.
Lieut. Cushing is wholly unknown
to me, and I see no reason that
would bring this case within the
meaning of Paragraph 32, Revised
Regulations of the Army.

B. S. Roberts
Bvt. Brig. Genl U.S.A.
+ St. Col. 3rd Cavalry,
Comdg. Regt.

Recd Sept. 10 - 67

EXHIBIT O cont.

Hd. Qrs. 3d U.S. Cav.
Fort Union, N.M. June 10 1867
Respectfully returned to the Adjutant General U.S.A. As it is at this
time more than probable that Lt.
Cushing, is a 1st Lieutenant in
his own Regiment, & as there is
no 1st Lieutenant in the 3d U.S.
Cavalry asking a transfer with
him, the transfer asked, would
seem to be contrary to the spirit
of par. No 30. Revised Army Regulations
for 1863. - The "cogent reasons" for the
transfer, as required by par. 32. of
the same Regulations are not given.
With the above objections, & from the
fact that there are no reasons given for
the transfer & on account of the earnestness shown by Maj. Thomas, without
supporting his earnestness with any
thing in. Lt. Cushings favor, I, as
Regt'l Commander object to said
transfer

(over)

BIBLIOGRAPHY

BOOKS

Altshuler, Constance Wynn. *Cavalry Yellow and Infantry Blue, Army Officers in Arizona Between 1851 and 1884*, Tucson: Arizona Historical Society, 1991.

------. *Chains of Command, Arizona and the Army, 1856-1875*, Tucson: Arizona Historical Society, 1981.

------. *Starting With Defiance, Nineteenth Century Arizona Military Posts*, Tucson: Arizona Historical Society, 1983.

Ball, Eve with Nora Hern and Linda Sanchez. *Indeh, an Apache Odyssey*, Provo: Brigham Young University Press, 1980.

Barnes, Will. *Arizona Place Names*, Revised and enlarged by Byrd H. Granger, Tucson: University of Arizona Press, Sixth Printing, 1977.

Boatner, Mark III. *The Civil War Dictionary*, New York: David McKay Company, Inc., 1988.

Bourke, John G. *On the Border With Crook*, New York: Charles Scribner's Sons, 1891, Reprinted by the University of Nebraska Press, Lincoln, 1971.

Coffman, Edward. *The Old Army, A Portrait of the American Army in Peace-time, 1874-1898*, New York, Oxford: Oxford University Press, 1986.

Downey, Fairfax. *Indian Fighting Army*, New York: Bantam Books, 1957.

------. *Sound of the Guns*, New York: David McKay Company, Inc., 1988.

Foner, Jack D. *The United States Soldier Between Two Wars: Army Life and Reforms*, New York: Humanities Press, 1970.

Giese, Dale F. *Echoes of the Bugle*, Silver City, N.M.: Phelps Dodge Corp., 1991.

Gustafson, A.M. ed. *John Spring's Arizona*, Tucson: University of Arizona Press, 1966.

Haight, Theron. *Three Wisconsin Cushings*, Milwaukee: Wisconsin History Commission, 1910.

Hodge, Frederick, ed. *Handbook of American Indians*, Totona, N.Y.: Rowan and Littlefield, 1975.

James, Gregory and the Editors of Time-Life Books. *The Killing Ground, Wilderness to Cold Harbor*, Alexandria, VA.: Time-Life Books, 1986.

Johnson, Swafford. *History of the United States Cavalry*, Greenwich, CT.: Bison Books Corp., 1985.

Lockwood, Frank C. *The Apache Indians*, Lincoln and London: University of Nebraska Press, 1938

Marszalek, John. *Sherman, a Solider's Passion for Order*, New York: The Free Press, A Division of MacMillen, Inc., 1993.

Martin, David. *The Shiloh Campaign, March-April 1862*, New York: Fairfax Press, 1987.

Mauncy, Albert. *Artillery Through the Ages*, Washington: National Park Service, 1949. (Reprint, 1985)

Morris, Ray Jr. *Sheridan, The Life and Wars of General Phillip Sheridan*, New York: Crown Publishing Company, 1992.

Porter, Joseph. *Paper Medicine Man, John Gregory Bourke and His American West*, Norman and London: University of Oklahoma Press, 1986.

Rickey, Don. *Forty Miles a Day on Beans and Hay*, Norman and London: University of Oklahoma Press, 1963

Roberts, Joseph. *The Hand Book of Artillery*, Tenth Edition, New York: D. Van Nostrand Co., Inc. 1975.

Roskie, Ralph and Van Doren, Charles. *Lincoln's Commando*, New York: Harper Brothers, 1957.

Thrapp, Dan. *Encyclopedia of Frontier Biography*, Glendale, CA.: Arthur H. Clark Co., 1988.

------. *Juh, An Incredible Indian*, El Paso: Texas Western Press, University of Texas at El Paso, 1973.

------. *The Conquest of Apacheria*, Norman and London, University of Oklahoma Press, 1967.

Urwin, Gregory. *The History of the United States Cavalry, an Illustrated History*, Dorset, England: Blandford Press, 1983.

Utley, Robert. *Frontier Regulars, The United States Army and the Indian, 1866-1890*, New York: MacMillen Publishing Company, Inc., 1973.

------. *The Indian Frontier of the American West*, Albuquerque: University of New Mexico Press, 1984.

Wheller, Richard. *The Siege of Vicksburg*, New York: Thomas Crowell Co., 1978.

Worcester, Donald. *The Apaches, Eagles of the Southwest*, Norman and London: University of Oklahoma Press, 1979.

Wormser, Richard. *The Yellowlegs, The Story of the United States Cavalry*, Garden City, N.Y.: Doubleday and Company, Inc., 1966.

GOVERNMENT PUBLICATIONS

Adjutant General's Office. *Chronological List of Actions, etc. With Indians From January, 1837, to January, 1891*, Introduction by Dale E. Floyd, Fort Collins, Co.: Old Army Press, 1979.

Report of the Adjutant General of the State of Illinois, Volume VIII, Containing Reports for the years 1861-1866, revised by Brigadier General J.N. Reese, Adjutant General, Springfield: Journal Company, 1901.

Revised United States Army Regulations of 1861 With an Appendix Containing the Laws Affecting Army Regulations and Articles of War to June, 1863, Washington: Government Printing House, 1863.

The War of the Rebellion, A Compilation of the Official Records of the Union and Conference Armies, Washington: Government Printing House, 1897.

NATIONAL ARCHIVES

Bimonthly Muster Reports, Third Cavalry, Troop F, September 30, 1868 to June 30, 1871.

Court Martial Proceedings, Case MM3549 (H.B. Cushing) Box 1416.

Department of Arizona, Special Order No. 74, August 9, 1870.

File for First Lieutenant Howard Cushing (9W3/18/2/C) Box 27.

Findings of the Court of Inquiry (Thomas, King) Case Number 3265, Box 1350.

Regimental Returns, First Illinois Light Artillery, Company B, November, 1861 to December, 1867. (8W3/14/35/B) Box 109.

Reports of the First United States Artillery, December, 1863, to September, 1867, Micro Copy Number 722, Roll Number 29.

Returns from United States Army Regiments, Third Cavalry, February, 1869, to June, 1871.

Returns from United States Military Posts:

-----Camp Crittenden, Arizona Territory.

-----Camp Grant, Arizona Territory.

-----Camp Lowell, Arizona Territory.

Special Order No. 112, Headquarters, Inspector of Artillery, United States Army, September 4, 1864.

Special Order No. 437, Headquarters of the Army, Adjutant General's Office, September 7, 1867.

NEWSPAPERS AND JOURNALS

Arizona Citizen
Army-Navy Journal
Boston Post Express
Fredonia Censor
Journal of the Military Service Institution of the United States

MAPS

Atlas to Accompany the Official Records of the Union and Confederate Armies, 1861-1865, Washington: Government Printing Office, 1891-1895.

Historical Atlas of Arizona, Second Edition, by Henry P. Walker and Don Bufkin, Norman and London: University of Oklahoma Press, 1986.

United States Department of the Interior, Geological Survey, Fifteen Minute Series, Fort Huachuca Quadrangle.

INDEX

Author Kenneth Randall is a native of Norristown, Pennsylvania and a retired teacher, coach and administrator with schools in that state.

He and his wife Peggy, live in Tucson. In addition to his passion for researching Arizona Territory frontier history, he is a docent at the Fort Lowell Museum, Tucson, Arizona.